THE 7 PRINCIPLES OF COMPLETE CO-CREATION

Stefanie Jansen

Maarten Pieters

BIS Publishers

Building Het Sieraad

Postjesweg 1

1057 DT Amsterdam

The Netherlands

T +31 (0)20 515 02 30

bis@bispublishers.com

www.bispublishers.com

ISBN 978 90 6369 473 9

Illustrations by Peter Guldemond

CONTENTS

READING GUIDE

This book explains the seven principles of complete co-creation:

Principle 1: together
Complete co-creation is based on equal collaboration between all relevant internal and external parties.

Principle 2: with end-users
In complete co-creation, end-users always play a central role.

Principle 3: ongoing
End-users and other relevant parties participate consistently in every phase of the complete co-creation process.

Principle 4: productive
Complete co-creation leads to implementation of the co-created solution.

Principle 5: transparant
In complete co-creation, relevant information is accessible to all participants.

Principle 6: supported
Complete co-creation is supported by all involved parties.

Principle 7: value-driven
Complete co-creation results in value creation for end-users, the involved organizations, and the planet.

The book has eight chapters: first a general introduction to co-creation and then seven chapters each dealing with one principle of complete co-creation. Because the seven principles are all interrelated, every chapter contains referrals to other chapters.
Each chapter is divided into several paragraphs answering practical questions about complete co-creation. Throughout the book you will find boxes with various case-studies and visions. Every chapter concludes with three questions meant to evoke our readers to translate the contents to their work reality.

In this book we will answer the following questions:

Introduction
1. What is complete co-creation and what is it not?
2. What are the three C's for effect maximization?
3. What is the Power Paradigm and why does it need to be replaced?
4. What is the Co-creation Paradigm and why does it suit our time?
5. What are drivers and barriers for embracing complete co-creation?
6. When is complete co-creation suitable?
7. Why follow the seven principles of complete co-creation?

Principle 1
8. Which parties to involve in complete co-creation?
9. What are the prerequisites for productive collaboration?

Principle 2
10. Why is it important for organizations to give end-users an active role?
11. What does active end-user involvement look like?
12. How to find, activate, and reward end-users?
13. Can other methods replace end-user contact?

Principle 3
14. What does a process of complete co-creation roughly look like?
15. What are the co-creative elements of phase 1, founding?
16. What are the co-creative elements of phase 2, finding?
17. What are the co-creative elements of phase 3, forming?
18. What are the co-creative elements of phase 4, fine-tuning?
19. What are the co-creative elements of phase 5, following up?

Principle 4
20. What are the main characteristics of a competent Co-creator?
21. How to empower the Co-creator?
22. How to support the Co-creator during fine-tuning and implementation?
23. How to deal with a lack of enthusiasm among stakeholders and key players?
24. How to prevent getting stuck in research or development?
25. How to prevent priority shifting?

Principle 5

26. Why is the black box a structural misfit with complete co-creation?
27. How does transparency relate to complete co-creation?

Principle 6

28. How to promote support for complete co-creation?
29. How to overcome barriers against supporting complete co-creation?

Principle 7

30. How do co-creative organizations create value on the level of end-users?
31. How do co-creative organizations create value on an organizational level?
32. How do co-creative organizations create value on the level of the planet?

PREFACE

Dear reader,

We are delighted that you have picked up our book, since we are well aware that its only right of existence is your interest for it. Before you start reading, we would like to share with you the story of the unlikely co-creation of The Seven Principles of Complete Co-creation.

We first met in the summer of 2010, when an educational publisher invited us to join efforts in the co-creation of a new method for teaching English to Dutch primary school kids.[1] That was an awfully cool assignment and it was successfully completed, too. However, in between that first meeting and the actual market launch, the co-creation team had to overcome pretty much every barrier against co-creation mentioned in this book.[2] We were only able to keep going because the top management of the involved organizations always had our backs.[3] At the same time, it was one of the most rewarding and fun co-creation trajectories in both our careers so far. Who gets to play SingStar[4] on the job with a bunch of groovy kids?!

In the fall of 2012, the same publisher invited us to the celebration of the method's early success. That night, we decided to found TheCoCreators. This was followed by long conversations about what co-creation really is and might become, and how TheCoCreators could help take it to the next level. To make our vision tangible, we created our website, conducted several co-creation trajectories, and developed our workshop "Introduction to Complete Co-creation". We also wrote some articles and blogs on the topic, launched our LinkedIn group, and spoke on various conferences.[5] At the same time, we defined a challenge: to add value to a market dominated by academic texts and case studies by means of a book offering a comprehensive, practical framework for co-creation.

The process from defining the challenge until having our book published was not a smooth ride. Maybe it was never meant to be. Looking back, it is from overcoming barriers that we have learned the most. Sometimes, these were barriers that pertained to the book directly. More often, though, they were only loosely related. In fact, the most daunting barriers had to do with our private situations. How do you keep on writing a book when you are moving abroad, getting married, becoming a parent, breaking up, or starting a new full-time job?

Well, it turns out that in times like that, you stop writing, and focus on what is more important. Then, when the storm is (more or less) over, you pick up right where you left. This is where it really helps to be on a team!

Once you realize that you were always in it together, and that you owe it to your work buddies to never give up, you will keep going. So we got it done. We still have a hard time believing it, but the proof is in your hands!

We co-created this book for those who, like ourselves, are set on adding sustainable value to their organization, the end-users, and our beautiful planet. For those who ambitiously want to be the change and humbly admit that they are only holding a small part of the puzzle. If you recognize yourself in this profile, keep reading and as you are going, please give us your honest feedback.

Thank you in advance for reading our book and sharing your ideas with us,

Stefanie Jansen   Maarten Pieters

---

1   More information on this case can be found in the introduction of this book.

2   In this particular co-creation trajectory, Maarten Pieters and Stefanie Jansen were members of a multidisciplinary co-creation team. The chapter dealing with principle 1 (together) explains what exactly a co-creation team is.

3   The chapter dealing with principle 6 (supported) mentions the potential barriers against co-creation and explains how to overcome them, as well as the importance of support and how to get it.

4   SingStar is a karaoke game, which was very popular in 2010: https://www.singstar.com/home.html

5   Our website (www.thecocreators.com) lists our publications. Our linkedIn group (TheCoCreators: Co-creation Network & Discussion Group) is now the world's largest co-creation group.

> The authors have succeeded in providing us all, who are involved in developing products, services, experiences, brands, and organizations of all sizes and complexities, with a powerful set of tools and references to leverage all of the potential of what they call 'complete co-creation'. The book provides a solid, result-oriented approach to tackling any challenge, that when practiced well, will undoubtedly change the way you look at getting to a solution. It will also effectively transform the way you organize your interactions with all of your stakeholders, including your end-users. Personally, I feel lucky to have recently become familiar with this book and I strongly believe I will be, in many ways, a better and more insightful designer through my exposure to and practice of complete co-creation!"
>
> *Pierre-Yves Panis, Chief Design Officer, Philips Lighting*

> In 2009, prof. Dr. Jacques Allegro formed an eclectic team with retired residents of his Amsterdam neighborhood. Supported by local politicians, a local branch of a large bank, and several local SME's, this team co-created Stadsdorpzuid (City Village South), a community for senior citizens wanting to grow older in the comfort of their own homes. Eight years later, we are with 425 members, helping each other while sharing a good time together. Our City Village keeps growing and evolving to best cater to our members' needs. We didn't realize it at the time, but while editing the Dutch version of The Seven Principles of Complete Co-creation, I learned that we were, and still are, intuitively working according to the principles of complete co-creation. That explains our success!"
>
> *Kees Jansen, former senior policy advisor for the City of Amsterdam,*
> *now member of the board of StadsdorpZuid*

> For most of my career, I have been working for organizations focusing on children as their end-users – from LEGO, Nickelodeon, and Spilgames, to WPG Kids. Over time, I have learned to always actively involve kids in every phase of new product and idea development, and to treat them as equal conversation partners. Their problem solving ability never ceases to amaze me. In their unbounded thinking, they come up with solutions and ideas that we, as grown-ups, have become blind to. This is why I view complete co-creation as a prerequisite for developing successful kids concepts. After having read The Seven Principles of Complete Co-creation, I have become convinced that this is true for any target group."
>
> *Dieneke Kuijpers, Directeur WPG Kindermedia*

INTRODUCTION

We are in the middle of a paradigm shift. For decades, our world followed the rules of what we call the 'Power Paradigm'. Recent years, however, reflect a growing realization that we can accomplish more together than alone, and that sharing leads to better solutions, better experiences, and ultimately to a better world. This is driving more and more individuals, groups, and organizations to change their ways. The ambition to work towards a better world not only gives rise to fierce criticism of the singular focus on profit growth that characterizes many large corporations, but also to a new paradigm: the 'Co-creation Paradigm'.

Thanks to information technology and modern ways of communication, the larger public can inform themselves – now more than ever – about pretty much anything. Moreover, the yields of any quest for information, as well as any attached opinions, can be instantly shared with the world. People directly exchange positive and negative stories about organizations and governments through social media and anyone can start an online petition. Reaching a critical mass to influence powerful institutions is easier now than it has ever been throughout history.

Communicating about or in the name of a particular group of people works less and less well; communicating *with* them is what works. Take this a step further and we find ourselves *creating with* citizens or consumers: co-creation.

Co-creation rising

The popularity of co-creation is quickly growing, and with good reason: co-creation leads to results! Products developed in co-creation with consumers score relatively high on the dimensions of 'relevance', and 'fulfills personal needs'.[1] Furthermore, products with the claim 'developed with consumers' sell significantly better than products without this claim.[2]

Structural, constructive collaboration with the intended end-users is a central element of what we call *complete co-creation*. Continuous collaboration with end-users distinguishes complete co-creation of 1) other ways to solve challenges, 2) various forms of target group connection, including market research, and 3) other forms of co-creation. Other forms of co-creation are the collaboration of organizations, as well as of departments within an organization, without active involvement of end-users.

> ❝ *Co-creation works because even the greatest creative rarely knows the complete answer – usually they know part of it or have a hunch. Someone somewhere probably knows another part of the solution, and so on, until a complete picture appears. By collaborating, we get to the solution quicker, and often with more elegance."*
> *John Williams, co-founder of WikiSolutions*[3]

1. More information about the quoted research done by InSites Consulting in collaboration with Heinz, R&D in 2011, can be found here: http://bit.ly/2wVSBdA

2. Van Dijk, J. (2011). The Effects of Co-creation on Brand and Product Perceptions. MSc thesis, Faculty of Social Sciences, Universiteit van Wageningen.

3. From the article Co-creation is the new Crowdsourcing, The Guardian (July 2013). This article has been removed by The Guardian. The same quote returns in the online article What Co-creation looks like: a future-making Primer: http://bit.ly/2wor7ZY

About the terminology in this book

Several terms keep coming back in this book. These terms have different meanings in different publications, depending on the author using them. To avoid ambiguity, we define them within the scope of this book.

Challenges and solutions

We will use the term 'solutions' when we refer to something that has been developed in co-creation. A solution can be anything: a new company, a new or revised product or service, an experience, or a communication. In the context of solutions we use the term 'challenges' which form the reason to start a co-creation trajectory. Since every problem can be viewed as a challenge, but not the other way around, we prefer the term 'challenge' over 'problem'.

End-users

End-users are the (intended) target group of the solution to be co-created: the people for whom the solution needs to be relevant and attractive to use. We prefer the term 'end-users' over 'consumers' because complete co-creation is also relevant for not-for-profit organizations and other organized groups that have no consumers, but do have end-users.

For business-to-business-organizations, the term end-users primarily refers to the buyers of their products and services, and secondarily to the end-users of the products and services of these buyers. For instance: organizations that deliver intermediate products can deem the organizations turning these intermediate products into final products as their end-users. However, the end-users may also be the people who use the final products. The context determines who the end-users are.

Organizations

In this book, the general term 'organization' includes all types of companies, initiatives, and groups that want to create value for certain end-users – whether these are profit or not-for-profit-organizations, business-to-consumer or business-to-business organizations. We often refer to the 'initiating organization' as the one starting a co-creation trajectory. Although other participating organizations can have a significant influence on the trajectory and may just as much be stakeholders in it, it is the initiating organization which carries the end-responsibility for the process and its yield.

The cases in this book

In this book we regularly use cases to illustrate certain premises. Although co-creation is the central topic of the book, not all cases are co-creation examples. Some illustrate a related issue, such as the use of social media to engage in dialogue with end-users or crowdsourcing to get to new ideas.

Reading guide for the introduction

This chapter is an introduction to the definition and backgrounds of 'complete co-creation'. Thus, we will answer the following crucial questions:

1. What is complete co-creation and what is it not?
2. What are the three C's for effect maximization?
3. What is the Power Paradigm and why does it need to be replaced?
4. What is the Co-creation Paradigm and why does it suit our time?
5. What are drivers and barriers for embracing complete co-creation?
6. When is complete co-creation suitable?
7. Why follow the seven principles of complete co-creation?

> ❝ *You should understand the power of the phenomenon [of user contribution] and, as I have, learn from the growing number of companies in traditional industries — firms like Honda, Procter & Gamble, Best Buy, and Hyatt — that are tapping user contributions to improve products, better serve customers, generate new business, reduce costs, boost employee performance, and more. Contribution-driven results like those are achievable for pretty much any business."*
> *Scott Cook, co-founder and chairman of the board of directors of Intuit[4] / member of the boards of directors of Procter & Gamble and eBay[5]*

1. What is complete co-creation and what is it not?

Recent years have witnessed an increase of people thinking and writing about co-creation. To the seemingly unequivocal label of 'co-creation', authors appoint many different things. These vary from market research to crowdsourcing, from design thinking[6] to open innovation, and from participating research to organizational collaboration.

Aiming to create clarity in this conceptual swamp, we coined the term 'complete co-creation' in 2013.[7] Whereas co-creation can include many different things, which are not always

---

4. Intuit is a company for financial software and web services in Mountain View, California.

5. As quoted in the article: The Contribution Revolution – Letting Volunteers Build your Business, Harvard Business Review (issue 10/2008) http://bit.ly/2h2QfzB

6. More information about design thinking can be found here: Hurst, N (2013). Big corporations are buying design firms in droves. Wired Magazine (issue 05/05/2013) and http://www.wired.com/2013/05/accenture-fjord/ and http://dschool.stanford.edu/dgift/. The topic of design thinking versus co-creation is discussed later this chapter.

Confusion about co-creation

related to creating something together, complete co-creation is not only unambiguous, but also the highest attainable form of co-creation. Not all organizations claiming to work in co-creation are following the principles of *complete* co-creation.

Complete co-creation

Complete co-creation means actively involving end-users and other relevant parties in a development process, from the identification of a challenge to the implementation and tracking of its solution. Complete co-creation is foremost a *procedure* which may evolve into an *organizational principle*, and potentially even a *co-ownership*.

Definition and premises of complete co-creation

▸ **Complete co-creation is the transparent process of value creation in ongoing, productive collaboration with, and supported by all relevant parties, with end-users playing a central role.**

A central premise of complete co-creation is that neither the various organizations in a value chain, nor the end-users can reach the ideal solution to any challenge without collaborating. This is because involved organizations and end-users have complementary knowledge and skills. The knowledge of product development and design, markets, suppliers, and sales channels is embedded within organizations.

7.   Read more on FrankWatching.com: http://bit.ly/2xwQzkW

In addition, end-users possess the key to their deeper motivations, dreams, and fears. Moreover, only end-users can provide a competitor analysis from a client's perspective, know better than anyone how their decision making tree works, and can start word-of-mouth for the solution. This means that if all relevant parties – including the end-users – will work together on a given challenge, the solution will not only optimally serve the end-users' needs, but will also gain acceptance and involvement of all parties responsible for its success.

CASE 1

Groove.me – complete co-creation in elementary school[8]

As a new player in the Dutch educational market, publisher Blink wants to re-invent education to spark inspiration within children to learn. The first project to materialize this ambition was the development of a method English for the upper grades of Dutch elementary schools.

With teacher needs and wishes being the customary focal point for the development of an educational method, Blink wanted to start with children's motivations. Thus, the innovation team set out immersing themselves in the world of children to find out what role the English language plays in their lives, how they learn English, and what their drivers and barriers are to do so.

Soon, music emerged as a common theme: popular music is both the driver to learn English and the means to do it. The teacher and English method used at school are secondary players at best. "Our teacher actually sucks at English," was a frequent remark.

The translation to an activating teaching method based on popular English music – with a mainly coaching and stimulating role for the teacher – materialized relatively quickly. Although the first sketch evoked a variety of critical questions and reactions, both children and teachers responded with great enthusiasm and Blink decided to invest in further development.

A team of educational and software experts entered multiple co-creation cycles with children and teachers until a didactically sound, yet swinging teaching method was ready to launch, entirely based on the principle of learning for and through music.

Soon after its introduction in 2011, Groove.me proved to be one of the most successful launches of a new educational method in recent years. From the year of launch, one in two elementary schools buying a new education method English chose Groove.me. That equals a yearly market share of 50%, a percentage that Groove.me has been steadily meeting year after year. A remarkable accomplishment for a new, unknown, and small player in an already satisfied, conservative market, dominated by a few large, established publishers!

In a 2012 client satisfaction research 90% of the teachers indicated that Groove.me was meeting or exceeding their expectations. In a 2013 research teachers scored Groove.me with 8 points on a 10-point scale, observing that children learn English better and faster with Groove.me than before and are more motivated as well.[9]

Woordenschat

Leer eerst de betekenis en uitspraak van deze woorden.
Kun je het liedje al raden?

a	can	hell	join	of	sharing
above	countries	hope	kill	one	sky
all	die	hope	life	only	someday
am	do	hunger	living	or	you
and	dreamer	I	man	peace	
as	easy	I'm	may	peop	
be	for	if	need	poss	
below	greed	imagine	no	religi	
brotherhood	hard	in	not	say	too
but	heaven	is	nothing	say	try
us	will	wonder	world		

> Klik op een woord voor de vertaling, de juiste Engelse uitspraak en om jezelf te testen

Exercise taken from the first concept of Groove.me, used as stimulus material in the development phase.

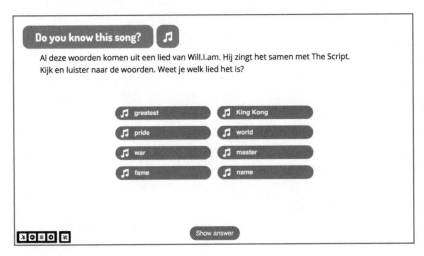

Do you know this song? ♫

Al deze woorden komen uit een lied van Will.I.am. Hij zingt het samen met The Script.
Kijk en luister naar de woorden. Weet je welk lied het is?

- ♫ greatest
- ♫ King Kong
- ♫ pride
- ♫ world
- ♫ war
- ♫ master
- ♫ fame
- ♫ name

Show answer

A real Groove.me exercise

8. Stefanie Jansen was involved in this case as an independent kids target group expert; Maarten Pieters as consultant of agency Flare Innovation (www.flare-innovation.com). The development process for Groove.me was conducted by Arjan Polhuijs, founder of Flare Innovation. More information on this case can be found here: http://bit.ly/2vTJK8s

9. More information on this case can be found here: http://www.thecocreators.com/case-study-groove-me/ and here: www.groove.me

Direct and indirect influence during complete co-creation

Complete co-creation does not mean that organizations share all decision making with end-users and other relevant parties. Boards of directors are responsible for the choices of the organization, also when it applies complete co-creation. Complete co-creation *does* imply, however, that end-users and other relevant parties are actively involved in different ways and in various organizational processes. That means they are of direct and indirect influence on decisions and developments.

Indirect influence works through information and inspiration provided by the diverse parties involved, each from their own unique perspective and knowledge frame. *Direct influence* works through concrete ideas and advice, as well as through active involvement in the primary process of the organization.

Complete co-creation as related to other types of creation

The main difference between complete co-creation and other ways to solve challenges is the productive collaboration between one or more organizations, end-users, and other relevant parties throughout the development process.

Unique characteristics of complete co-creation

The most distinguishing characteristic of complete co-creation is the *central role of end-users*. Activities focused on value creation that fail to involve end-users, do not qualify as complete co-creation. End-users can add to a co-creation process in different ways, online as well as offline. Think active participation in creative sessions, optimization sessions, creative briefs, presentations to stakeholders, etc.[10]

Another distinguishing characteristic is *productivity*. That refers to the premise that complete co-creation always leads to an implementable solution. When end-users and other relevant parties were involved, but failed to implement a concrete solution, the process does not qualify as complete co-creation.

Design thinking and complete co-creation

The popular movement of design thinking focuses on a creative, out of the box approach of challenges. User experience is its vantage point. Qualitative exploratory market research is the usual tool for gaining understanding of user experience, followed by concept testing.[11] Although design thinking is definitely a customer-centric approach and can very well be used to shape a complete co-creation trajectory, end-user involvement does not automatically make it co-creation. Only if end-users play an active, co-developing role in every step of the development process does design thinking fit the criteria for complete co-creation.

2. What are the three C's for effect maximization?

Customer connection – an ongoing relationship between organization and end-users – is a *precondition* for complete co-creation.[12] Customer insight – a deep understanding of end-users' motivations – is the central *guideline* for complete co-creation.[13] We refer to customer connection, customer insight, and complete co-creation as the three C's for effect maximization.

> 66 *Only when you really listen to youth you will understand what drives them. And that is often different than what you thought beforehand."*
> *Brigitte van Teeffelen, OKC-manager Amsterdam-Noord* [14]

Customer connection, customer insight, and complete co-creation

There are three reasons why consistent implementation of the three C's leads to effect maximization. First: organizations that maintain continuous contact with their end-users through various online and offline channels know the unmet needs in their market and can respond to these faster and with greater relevance than their less customer connected competitors. Second: organizations that take customer insight as a basis for their decision making are recognizable and attractive to their end-users. Third: organizations that structurally embrace customer connection, customer insight, and complete co-creation create maximum relevance for their end-users, which often comes with sympathy, resulting in end-user loyalty.

> 66 *I think there is an old adage that says something like: 'The customer is always right...' This is truer now than ever in the world of customization."*
> *Thomas Davis, worldwide head of e-commerce at PUMA*[15]

10. Principles 2 (with end-users) and 3 (ongoing) deal with how to involve end-users and their possible roles in a complete co-creation trajectory.

11. More information on design thinking and the importance of user experience can be found here: http://bit.ly/2xjpxMO

12. Principle 2 (with end-users) deals with customer connection.

13. Principle 7 (value-driven) deals with the term 'insight'.

14. OKC stands for Ouder en Kind Centra (Parent and Child Centers), the Amsterdam variety of the Dutch CJG's (Centers for Youth and Family). She said this during the evaluation of the development process of JIP Noord.

15. This quote comes from an interview with Embodee (july 2013). More information can be found here: http://bit.ly/2h1XStZ

The Customer Connection Pyramid

The Customer Connection Pyramid shows the development of organizations from customer connection through customer insight to complete co-creation. The pyramid visualizes how a solid basis of customer connection and customer insight needs to be founded before starting a co-creation trajectory, and that a good way to ease into complete co-creation is to first perform several co-creation pilots. Safe experiments with direct collaboration between organizations and end-users provide the needed trust to fully embrace complete co-creation.

The 3C's for effect maximization in the Customer Connection Pyramid

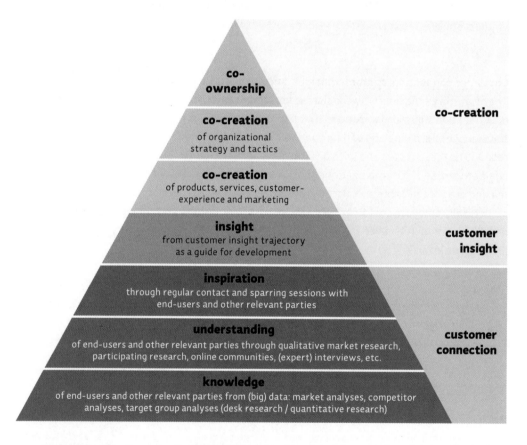

3. What is the Power Paradigm and why does it need to be replaced?

Since the industrial revolution, the most successful organizations have developed into gigantic imperia that aim to maintain market dominance by occupying strategic positions. These organizations flourish in what we call the Power Paradigm, in which success is defined by economical growth.

Duality opposes value creation

Duality is central to the Power Paradigm. Words that fit it: 'us-them', 'against', 'closed off', 'distrust', and 'organization profit'. Within this paradigm, knowledge sharing is dangerous because competitors can use this to create an even better product or to take over strategic positions. Thus, organizations focus on knowledge dominance, resulting in a unique asset that cannot be copied by others. This is contrary to the aim of adding true value to end-users and the planet.

CASE 2

Microsoft - Giant from the era of power

Founded in 1976 and expanded during the power paradigm, Microsoft is one of the most famous multinationals of our time. For most of its existence, Microsoft has been focused on establishing market dominance through knowledge dominance – not only in its primary market of operating software, but also in other markets that the company considered strategically crucial, for instance the market for game consoles and the mobile market.

Characteristic for the continuous fight for market dominance are the many lawsuits Microsoft has been involved in, such as those with Apple and with the federal government of the United States.[16] The latter wanted to force Microsoft to break into smaller organizations in order to prevent the company from realizing a market monopoly.

Another characteristic was Microsoft's secrecy. Strategy and innovation would be determined through internal processes. These were not transparent for the outside world, unless they would leak, which happened to the "Halloween Documents" in 1998. The Halloween Documents contained Microsoft's strategy in reaction to the rising of free and open source software, in particular Linux. With Microsoft's failure on the mobile market and the flop of Windows 8,[17] it seemed that the giant would slip as a result of its old-fashioned organizational focus. However, even this large tanker has shifted gear and started experimenting with co-creation.

Windows 10, developed in collaboration with millions of end-users, is doing a lot better than its predecessors. The system realized more than 350 million users within a year after launch, an adoption ratio that is much higher than those of all prior versions.[18]

16.   More information about the fights between Microsoft and Apple can be found here: http://zd.net/2wWtMy6

More information about the Halloween Documents can be found here: http://bit.ly/2y5yvvk

17.   More information on Windows can be found here: http://bit.ly/2xkehQr

18.   More information on the development of Windows 10 and its results can be found here: http://bit.ly/2wpF4Xu

Tendencies opposing the Power Paradigm

Various current-time tendencies are limiting the Power Paradigm's shelf life. We identify the following: the increase in knowledge leakage, the professionalization of the copy culture, the expansion of ways of getting around establishment and the growing importance of trust and added value on an individual level.

Knowledge dominance is becoming harder to maintain

The internet allows information to spread so fast that knowledge dominance can no longer be taken as a given. Organizational advantage based on long-term knowledge dominance can now be lost to competitors that have access to the same knowledge and are applying it in a more relevant way.

CASE 3

Old Nestlé-CEO introduces environmentally friendly Nespresso-cups[19]

Jean-Paul Gaillard, one of Nestlé's recent CEO's (1988 through 1997) and now owner of the Ethical Coffee Company, proves that competition by knowledge leakage can hit seemingly invincible market leaders where they least expect it. After leaving Nestlé, Gaillard went on to develop, produce, and market biodegradable capsules for the Nespresso-machines. These were a lot more environmentally friendly than the aluminum capsules produced by Nestlé. Nestlé changed the Nespresso-machines to where they were no longer compatible with Gaillard's capsules. In response, ECC successfully sued Nestlé.

Despite his legal success, Gaillard decided to abandon the coffee capsule market. Not only was the legal fight against his former employer financially draining, in addition ECC has not been able to secure a substantial distribution of their capsules in supermarkets. Moreover, the recent wave of new competitors in the market – the giant Starbucks amongst them – makes it difficult to stay profitable. ECC will seek other ways of adding value with environmentally friendly coffee products and is working on an innovation in the coffee segment.

Even with ECC pulling out of the coffee capsule market, Nestlé has a hard time maintaining its market dominance based on knowledge dominance and patents. In 2013, the organization already lost a crucial patent, giving way to more than 200 organizations to produce capsules for the Nespresso-machines for a lower price, and/or marketing their own, knock-off coffee-capsule-makers.[20]

19.   Adapted from: http://bit.ly/2h1xYCX and http://bit.ly/2x01phI

20.   More information about Nespresso throughout the years can be found here: http://bit.ly/2fh721F

Knowledge leakage happens in several ways. One way is job-hopping and head-hunting. Nowadays, few employees stay with the same company throughout their career. Although larger organizations often have agreements not to steal each other's employees, employee exchanges between competitors can't be entirely prevented. For instance, rumor has it that Apple – in response to its problems with the mobile maps application – deliberately targeted Google Maps employees.[21]

Another way is whistle-blowing. The new generation of whistle-blowers shares sensitive information with the world out of personal motives such as ethics, revenge, or sensationalism. This trend is related to the increasingly critical attitude of employees towards their employers, as well as with the fact that creating impact by sharing information was never this easy. A famous recent example is Edward Snowden, who leaked secret information of the NSA (the National Security Agency of the USA).[22]

A third threat to knowledge dominance is the trend of sharing. Recent years have witnessed various organizations blossom that are built on the premise that the free sharing of knowledge, ideas, and tools with the public will ultimately benefit all involved parties. An example is open source software, which allows anyone to read, adapt, and spread its source code. Firefox is a successful internet browser working according to this principle.[23]

> 66 *Many people may not realize it, but a lot of innovation such as*
> *big data and cloud arose from the open source community."*
> *Damien Wong, General Manager at Red Hat*[24]

The protective power of patents is ever more limited
Sooner or later, successful products and brands will be copied by companies specialized in creating copy-cats. Patents have ever limited protective power, not only because at some point they cease to be, but also because applying minimal amendments to the original is an easy way to circumvent them. Thus, product secrets are quickly losing their value. Expectations are that this trend will reach its tipping point once 3D-printers become widely accessible.

21. More information on Apple's mobile maps development can be found here: http://tcrn.ch/2wZLEFY
22. More information about the Snowden case can be found here: http://bit.ly/2y4Mod5
23. More information on Firefox can be found here: https://mzl.la/2h2ZXWB
24. Quote from: http://bit.ly/2f5V7Hf

Maintaining market dominance is increasingly difficult

In recent times, it was relatively easy to protect strategic positions by means of mass (money, men, material). Now, however, the laws have changed. Current consumers have access to the knowledge, means, and channels to go around the established suppliers. We can get anything online, straight from the manufacturer, and we can also use online platforms for leasing, borrowing, and exchanging to get the things and services we need – with closed wallets – directly from private people and businesses. Moreover, private production is a possibility that will quickly gain relevance, given the rapid rise of 3D-printing on demand. The choice of suppliers is more and more based *on trust*.

CASE 4

Success by sharing – Uber and Airbnb [25]

Recent years have witnessed new players that seem to arise out of nowhere and grow fast by suddenly changing the established rules. These newcomers play into their clients' need for a good deal with a trustworthy, likeable, and personal provider. This need is translated to a client-oriented service, without investing in market dominance based on owning assets. The two most famous organizations operating within this new principle are Airbnb and Uber. Airbnb is now the world's largest hotel service, without owning any hotels. Uber is the world's largest taxi service, without owning any cars.

On a global level, as well as locally, hotel chains and taxi organizations have tried to sabotage these new competitors – so far unsuccessfully. Ultimately, the client is king, and the client wants the combination of a sharp price with a personal approach and a good service. While the establishment continues to attack, Airbnb and Uber are reaping the fruits of their 'win-more-concept', allowing everyone to win: the service organization, the end-users, the private suppliers of beds and rides, and ultimately the planet. After all, intensifying the use of already existing houses and cars is very environmentally friendly.

However, in order to secure the long-term loyalty of their end-users, even successful starters need to stay close to their core values and should not get carried away by large profits. Both Uber and Airbnb have recently become the subject of criticism. For instance, Uber is being accused of not sharing enough of its profits with the taxi drivers, as well as failing to protect them against financial setbacks, while Airbnb is accused of not helping to prevent the exploitation of empty houses as hotels under its label. Time will tell whether these problems will disappear when the collaborative economy grows or whether it is a structural breaking with these organizations' own fundamental values. If it is the later, then this could give rise to competitors with greater integrity.

25. More information about the dark side of Uber and Airbnb can be found here: http://bit.ly/2xw7QKU, http://bit.ly/2w0wL9u, http://for.tn/2w76t5g ,and here: http://bit.ly/2f5zzdL

26. More information on the angora wool scandal can be found here: http://bit.ly/2xjRxjF

Consumer trust is becoming more important

Trust is not based on money and power, but on value, honesty, authenticity, involvement, transparency, and sympathy. Driven by the explosively growing accessible (online) information, end-users know more about organizations, their methods, and quality delivered. Quickly sharing negative information – such as manufacturers using carcinogenic ingredients, companies' unjust treatment of employees, and CEO's receiving unreasonably high bonuses – end-users have become increasingly critical and may even decide to boycott certain organizations. For instance, several action-groups have pushed large European retail chains such as H&M, Topshop, and Zara to remove products that products containing cruelly produced angora wool from their collections.[26]

Today's end-users want to see how organizations work, what they stand for, and how they create value for their employees, suppliers, and buyers. Organizations trying to maintain a dominant position by being secretive about their knowledge, internal processes, and strategic relations run the risk of losing their end-users' trust, thus giving way to competitors.

CASE 5

Triodos Bank, trustworthy beacon during the financial crisis[27]

Since the 2008 financial crisis, customer trust in the banking sector has dropped to an all-time low. The real threat of private people losing their stocks and savings in combination with the outrageous salaries, bonuses, and redundancy payments of CEO's in the sector have been fueling a general sense of distrust. Yet certain players flourish in this climate.

The Dutch Triodos Bank is a glorious example. Since the start of the financial crisis the bank has doubled its size and number of clients, and scored 'most reliable bank' three times in a row in the Customer Centric DNA research. Moreover, its balance total grew with 22%, the trusted capital with 20%, and the profits with 14%.[28] This is especially remarkable since the bank offers a lower interest rate and less user-convenience than some of its competitors.

From its foundation, Triodos has played into the growing realization that savings can add to a sustainable, social society. An extra impulse during the crisis was the bank's open management. Triodos publishes assigned credits on its website and transparently shows the public that it refrains from speculation, short-term investment, stock quotation, and sky-high profits. Thus fulfilling a central need for control, Triodos consistently manages to attract and keep clients, especially in times of uncertainty.

27.   More information about Triodos bank can be found here: http://bit.ly/2xYTYFo
28.   These numbers can be found here: http://bit.ly/2xYTYFo

Consumers are realizing that – ultimately – *they* have the power and not the corporations. Should all consumers decide to only spend money on products and services that perfectly fit their individual needs, without compromising our planet, they would push organizations into consistent, sustainable client-centeredness. This effect is starting to become visible in the western world. Financial crisis or not, the popularity of organic, sustainable, and fair trade products is on a steady rise, just like ethical banking, green energy, and energy-efficient appliances.

The mass-driven approach is less effective

Being able to create value for individual consumers is rapidly becoming the number one predictive factor for customer loyalty. Personalization of online applications and new technology such as 3D-printing, are making customization easier than ever before. This trend opposes mass production and diminishes the relevance of owning a superior product line or dominating strategic positions.

The focus on pushing the largest possible volume of independently produced products is shifting to 1) developing relevant propositions, 2) manufacturing these in a time and cost efficient way, and 3) distributing them efficiently. This makes collaboration with end-users and other relevant parties, such as designers, suppliers, sales channels, and specialists essential.

From mass communication to dialogue

Mass communication is a central element in the marketing machine of organizations flourishing in the Power Paradigm. It worked well when the sources of information were limited and advertisers knew exactly which media were used when, where, and with what frequency by which target groups. The media consumption of today's consumers, however, is not as predictable. Not only are there a lot more (online) media channels, there is also a lot more accessible content, especially when taking user-generated content into consideration.

Dialogue reaches more end-users more effectively than mass-communication

In the current overflowing media landscape, the odds that the intended target group will view a commercial at a certain TV-channel or read an ad in a certain magazine are extremely small. That explains why an increasing number of organizations are shifting their communication budget from mass media to dialogue with their end-users, mostly through social media. There is a growing realization that it works best to have end-users communicate their needs and try to fulfill these at an individual level, rather than aiming for a 'one size fits all' compromise.

KLM successfully embraces social media[29]

Over the past decade, social media usage has been growing exponentially. Research by comScore shows that in 2015, Europeans spent 22% of their online time on social media. In Latin-America this percentage was 29%, as compared to 14% in North-America, and 8% in Asia.[30] Reflecting this trend, 99% of the global brands are active on social media.[31] The Dutch airline company KLM is a successful pioneer in this field. KLM integrated several online platforms in its social media program and was the first organization in The Netherlands to offer clients 24-hour accessibility through social media. KLM's online strategy accelerated when the Icelandic volcano Eyjafjallajökull erupted in 2010. The telephone lines were red-hot with calls from stranded travelers, and the website barely managed to keep up with traffic. When KLM decided to use Facebook and Twitter as crisis communication channels, it was the only airline able to keep travelers up-to-date with the latest developments. KLM's social media approach is payed off with a higher client satisfaction, better service perception, and higher brand awareness outside of The Netherlands. Air France-KLM's 2014 Corporate Social Responsibility Report shows a 71% increase on Facebook up to 13.151.570 fans, a 79% increase on Twitter up to 2.163.485 followers, and a 287% increase on Instagram up to 157.841 followers.[32]

A growing number of end-users avoid mass-communication

In explaining the declining effects of mass communication, again, the rise of the internet is crucial. More than ever, end-users have access to exactly the content they like. They also have the power to shield themselves from information and communication they don't like, or to find counter-arguments. With critical TV-programs, documentaries, and online platforms acting as sources of self-education, today's end-users are more aware of marketing effects. They are better equipped to identify empty promises, choosing products and services that represent *real* value to them.[33]

4. What is the Co-creation Paradigm and why does it suit our time?

The accessibility of information about how politicians and organizations view the world and their contributions to our quality of life promote the realization that an honest, value-driven attitude is necessary for the future of humanity on Planet Earth. Not only politicians, but also spiritual leaders such as the Dalai Lama and the Pope, as well as celebrities such as

29. More information on the KLM case can be found here: http://bit.ly/2xYUfrU

30. More information on the comScore research can be found here: http://bit.ly/2x0L4cU

31. More information on trends in social media can be found here: http://bit.ly/2xZrGKI

32. The full report can be found here: http://bit.ly/2jmKHEz

33. More information on end-users' increasingly critical attitude can be found here: http://bit.ly/2x0bGck

Leonardo di Caprio keep voicing this message. This realization and the increased power of the masses call for a new paradigm based on inclusion rather than duality. We call that the Co-creation Paradigm, which has harmony, openness, and honesty as its central values.

The Co-creation Paradigm is emerging from a period characterized by a growing focus on client-centeredness in both profit and not-for-profit sectors. In recent years, more and more organizations have experimented with end-user collaboration so as to maximize the relevance of their products, services, customer experience, and marketing mix – co-creation as ultimate client-centeredness.

> 6️⃣ *Citizens and customers no longer serve as suppliers for information about their needs (as in traditional innovation management); they make contributions to the process of developing new products to resolve problems."*
> *Howald and Schwartz, researchers at TU Dortmund[34]*

Organizations operating within the Co-creation Paradigm have expanded their focus beyond profit growth. Aiming to create sustainable value, they seek structural collaboration with other organizations, experts, and end-users. Ramaswamy and Prahalad, the fathers of the thinking about co-creation, refer to this as 'win-more – win-more': co-creation helps manifest benefits for the organization, the end-users, and the planet.[35] Words that fit this paradigm: 'us', 'together', 'open', 'trust', and 'value creation'.

> 6️⃣ *Building effective social ecosystems requires going beyond "doing well by doing good" to "doing even better for ourselves by doing well for others." By creating more value with others, the "win more-win more" nature of co-creation, simultaneously generates enhanced wealth-welfare-wellbeing."*
> *Ramaswamy and Ozcan, Professors of Marketing at University of Michigan, and Marywood University*

The paradigm shift visualized in the Co-Creation Transition Model
The Co-creation Transition Model shows the shift from the Power Paradigm to the Co-creation Paradigm. The model illustrates how three important trends in our society lead to

34. More information about the research carried out by Howald and Schwartz (2010) can be found here: http://bit.ly/2eUycec

35. More information about the 'win more – win more principle' can be found here: Ramaswamy, V. & Gouillart, F. (2010). The Power of Co-Creation: Build It with Them to Boost Growth, Productivity, and Profits. New York: Free Press.

the transformation of an increasing number of organizations from organization-driven to value-driven.

In a typical transitional process, an organization sets out by sending less and sharing more. Then it will start exchanging dominance for collaboration. When finally the organization is ready to experiment with transparency, it leaves the Power Paradigm. This process mostly occurs within established organizations; In contrast, most recent startups tend to operate within the Co-creation Paradigm right off the bat.

The Co-creation Transition Model

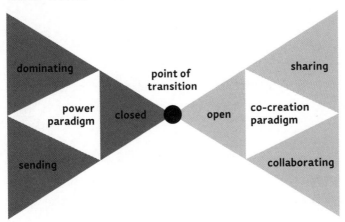

5. What are drivers and barriers for embracing complete co-creation?

Complete co-creation suits our time-frame and has unique benefits. However, not all organizations embrace it. To do so, there are usually a few barriers to overcome first.

Benefits of complete co-creation

Relevance
When the intended end-user group is consistently involved in *all* necessary steps in a development process, the output will be relevant, recognizable, and attractive for this group.

Marketing
The involved end-users will spread word among their peers about the development process long before it yields a solution. This will give the market introduction a boost. Moreover, in a complete co-creation process, end-users play an active role in developing marketing instruments, thus increasing their effectiveness. Finally, claiming end-user involvement can increase the credibility of the co-created solution's benefits.

Motivation

From the very beginning it is evident to everyone involved why, for whom, and how the development process will take place. This in combination with its open, interactive character will instill the awareness of "by me, through me, for me" among all participants. Furthermore, taking end-users' perspective as a vantage point will have a motivating effect because it provides a clear mission: "why and for whom are we doing this".

> 66 *Developing a service with, for, and by youth is fun;*
> *it gives all involved parties energy!"*
> Laura Kamphaus, policy advisor of the Dutch county IJsselstein

Efficiency

Because the process does not allow for decisions based on non-validated assumptions, repeating phases or steps is not necessary. That prevents wasting time and money.

Result

The co-created solution optimally suits end-users' needs and wishes, which – on the longer term – will lead to results beyond just the financial aspects. These may include spontaneous word of mouth and end-user loyalty.

Barriers against complete co-creation

Many organizations still favor other guidelines over the principles of complete co-creation. They may organize an internal brainstorm without end-users or hire an innovation agency which delivers a full-fledged concept, potentially claiming that end-users had a say in its development. Refraining from co-creation may stem from a lack of knowledge about it. This is getting less common, though, as awareness of co-creation is rapidly spreading. However, knowing about co-creation is not enough to embrace it as the new reality.[36]
In order to do that, trust that it will lead to success is necessary.

> 66 *Risk perception is the root of the general lack of enthusiasm for change. Change*
> *activates an ancient instinct related to perceived risks, especially when the involved people*
> *already had bad experiences with change in the past. Because co-creation is a new way of*
> *thinking and doing for most organizations, you can see it as change. The most important*
> *barrier against accepting co-creation as a new reality is risk perception: the risk of the*
> *destination, the risk of the journey, and the risk related to letting go of the old ways."*
> Olaf Hermans, Customer Goodwill Strategist at SiR-Intel

6. When is complete co-creation suitable?

Complete co-creation can be useful in all types of organizations during the entire development process of any solution, related to any challenge. This is true for challenges close to end-users, as well as for challenges further removed from them.

Complete co-creation is relevant for all types of organizations

We have witnessed complete co-creation work its magic for startups and multinationals, profit and non-profit organizations, business-to-business and business-to-consumer organizations. From retailers to toy manufacturers, from the food industry to government institutions, from health care to publishers and electronics – all branches can profit from complete co-creation, because creating end-user loyalty and support among other important parties is relevant for all.

Complete co-creation is possible in various stages of development

Complete co-creation is applicable during the entire development process of any solution for any challenge – from the creation of something new to the improvement, personification, or communication of something that already exists. It encompasses all steps in a development process: from the identification of a challenge to the introduction and monitoring of its solution.

Complete co-creation works for challenges close to and removed from end-users

Most organizations use co-creation for challenges close to end-users, particularly product innovation. Its principles are hardly being applied to challenges that are further removed, such as the strategic development of future scenarios, the determination of a long-term strategy, or the streamlining of organizational processes. We are convinced that complete co-creation is also relevant for such challenges, since end-users and other relevant parties can add a unique perspective in these instances, too. We expect that such examples will be easier to find in the near future, as we are just at the beginning of the co-creation revolution.

VISION

Tomorrow's customers expect to be taken seriously as equal partners
Our frequent work with children shows that sparring with organizations comes natural to the younger generations. They find it logical that organizations take their opinion into consideration when determining their strategies, especially when it concerns products for children, but also when

36. Principle 6 (supported) deals with barriers against co-creation and how to deal with them.

it concerns 'their' world of tomorrow. Children appreciate organizations reaching out to them and like to get to know the people that work there. Moreover, they are curious to look inside offices and factories, learn how innovations are realized, what the CEO's favorite food is, and how organizations are adding to a better world.

When in research for new kids' cookies, children were confronted with concepts for games on the website an eleven-year-old boy suggested that the website instead show what really happens in the cookie factory and who works there.

In a research for an educational magazine, children suggested that the publisher explain on TV how she develops new items and what the role of children is in this process.

After a brainstorm session for a new kids event children said they expected the organization to really use their ideas and that they would love to be involved in running the event.

In a brainstorm session for a kid-friendly supermarket, children not only came up with ideas to add play value to the supermarket, but also developed innovative concepts to have the supermarket operate in an environmentally friendly way, and how surplus products could be funneled to poor people and the homeless.

Our work with adolescents and young adults does not lead us to believe that the wish to be taken seriously and have an influence on the organizations around them should decline with age. On the contrary: various research shows that youth and young adults embrace brands that take them serious and a 2010 research shows that 40% of the 16-34 year-olds feel that brands are not taking them serious enough.[37] More than the generations before them, today's young adults choose to be self-employed as they don't want to conform to an organization with principles that aren't theirs.[38] A growing number of youth and young adults are seeking space to shape their own ideas in freedom and thus influence the world around them.

7. Why follow the seven principles of complete co-creation?

The seven principles of complete co-creation describe the prerequisites necessary for a development process to be called complete co-creation. They are derived from the definition: *complete co-creation is the transparent process of value creation in ongoing, productive collaboration with, and supported by all relevant parties, with end-users playing a central role.*

1. **Together.** Complete co-creation is based on equal collaboration between all relevant internal and external parties.
2. **With end-users.** In complete co-creation, end-users always play a central role.
3. **Ongoing.** End-users and other relevant parties participate consistently in every phase of the complete co-creation process.
4. **Productive**. Complete co-creation leads to implementation of the co-created solution.

5. **Transparent.** In complete co-creation, relevant information is accessible to all participants.
6. **Supported.** Complete co-creation is supported by all involved parties.
7. **Value-driven.** Complete co-creation results in value creation for end-users, the involved organizations, and the planet.

The case study JIP Noord encompasses all seven principles. This is why this case returns in every chapter, every time in light of the principle of complete co-creation that is the topic of that chapter.

CASE 7

JIP Noord was developed for and by local youth with various other parties[39]

In 2011 the quarter Amsterdam-Noord started with the development of a local information service for youth. Astrid Krikken, the responsible senior policy advisor, and Brigitte van Teeffelen, the OKC-manager[40], hired Martine Jansen as an external Co-creator. Her first step was to conduct an extensive research to gain insight into the needs and wishes of local youth aged 12 through 23. Interviews were carried out with random youth in local public transport, as well as round table meetings with groups of youth. In addition, the local Youth Council carried out an online quantitative survey among local youth. Finally, Martine interviewed all potential partners and stakeholders – from local youth and street work to the police – to learn from their experience and ideas.
The research yielded a list of do's and don'ts for developing the information service. A broad cross-section of local youth and stakeholders gave their feedback to this list, after which some of them formed a co-creation team that came up with a concept, verbalized as well as visualized.
This co-creation team of youth and involved parties called the conceptual service JIP Noord. JIP stands for Youth Information Point and is an abbreviation commonly used for information services. Involved youth presented the concept to the local alderman, policy advisors, and all potential partners.

37. More information on youth and brands can be found here: http://bit.ly/2fhHCRD, http://bit.ly/2xwYoHi, and here: http://bit.ly/2w8vvRC

38. More information about the current generation of youth and young adults and their relation to work can be found here http://bit.ly/2fh9OUD, and here: http://bit.ly/2xkiEej

39. As a self-employed member of De JeugdZaak, Martine Jansen was affiliated with de JeugdZaak and hired as JIP Noord Co-creator. She hired Stefanie Jansen on several occasions as a researcher and moderator. Read more here: http://bit.ly/2x0CFpM

40. The abbreviation OKC stands for Ouder en Kind Centrum (Parent and Child Center). OKC's were varieties of the Dutch CJG's (Centers for Youth and Family) in Amsterdam. Nowadays, Amsterdam has mobile OKT's (Parent and Child Teams).

After the development of JIP Noord was officially approved, the co-creation team briefed an architect for the interior decoration of the physical information center and a designer for the development of the logo and look and feel of the website. Furthermore, the team helped with the construction of website texts and flyers, and worked in information stands about JIP Noord at schools for secondary education. The result was that the involved youth inadvertently spread their enthusiasm for JIP Noord to their peers long before the actual location opened its doors. Obviously, youth played a large role at that opening, and stayed involved in operating JIP Noord afterwards. Whereas other youth information services often struggle with attracting visitors, visitor numbers for JIP Noord were high right from the start, online as well as offline. Seven months after opening JIP Noord had effectively helped more than 3000 youth, of whom 750 physically at the center itself, and the rest mainly through WhatsApp, email, and telephone. Apart from common themes such as education, work, and housing, a lot or their questions had to do with issues that youth normally don't speak freely about, such as debts, sexuality, and domestic violence. A quarter of the youth helped at JIP Noord came from outside of the area.

By involving youth and local partners in every step of the development process as co-producers, evaluators, and ultimately as JIP Noord personnel, the quarter Amsterdam-Noord has created a beautiful example of complete co-creation.

The co-creative organization

We call organizations that have fully integrated the seven principles of complete co-creation: 'co-creative organizations'. They regularly make analyses of data, derived from the combination of continuous customer connection and an ongoing evaluation of the implemented solutions. Thus, they always have an up-to-date list of challenges that are suitable for complete co-creation, and tend to have several co-creation trajectories running at the same time.

Embracing adventure

Complete co-creation is an adventure calling for openness, curiosity, overcoming fear, and letting go of the need to control. This may seem scary or simply unacceptable for those used to work according to detailed, planned, linear processes with a predetermined outcome. However, once the barriers have been overcome and the seven principles adopted as the new way of thinking and working, complete co-creation will quickly prove itself as a quick, relatively cheap, and inspiring way to sustainable success, well suited for the specific challenges of our time. Once a co-creator, forever a co-creator!

> *Co-creation is a 'way of life'. Only when you fully integrate co-creation in your organization's processes you will learn its value."*
> *Dieneke Kuijpers, Director at WPG Kindermedia*

8. Questions to our readers

1. Which advantages of complete co-creation are most relevant for your organization?

2. Where in the Customer Connection Pyramid is your organization, and what does it need to rise a little higher?

3. Where would you place your organization in the shift of Power Paradigm to Co-creation Paradigm?

a. entirely in the Power Paradigm
b. starting to transition to the Co-creation Paradigm
c. mostly transformed to the Co-creation Paradigm
d. entirely in the Co-creation Paradigm

Complete co-creation is
based on equal collaboration
between all relevant internal
and external parties.

PRINCIPLE 1
TOGETHER

Co-creation follows from the premise that organizations, end-users and other relevant parties need each other to get to the ideal output. That is because everyone has complementary skills and knowledge. Only a concerted effort of *all* directly and indirectly involved parties leads to completion of the entire puzzle. We call this the 'puzzle principle'. The rigorous application of this principle results in productive collaboration between the initiating organization, end-users, and all involved parties, such as suppliers, sales channels, experts, and possibly even competitors.

> *Innovation has always been a group activity. The myth of the lone genius having a Eureka moment that changes the world is indeed a myth. Most innovation is the result of long hours building on the input of others... If you are comfortable with the language of memes, you could say a healthy meme needs an ecosystem not of a single brain, but of a network of brains. That's how ideas bump into other ideas, replicate, mutate, and evolve."*
> *Chris Anderson, TED Curator*[1]

When people are working together in order to create real value, they engage in what we call 'productive collaboration'.[2] For productive collaboration to occur it is important that all relevant parties are included. Both adding irrelevant parties and not including certain parties who do have a crucial point of view can result in counter-productive collaboration, not yielding any real value.

Including all relevant parties is not enough; skillful guidance by a competent process owner is necessary for value creation to take place. This key figure is often referred to as the project manager, innovation manager or project coordinator. We use the name Co-creator, alternating between 'he' and 'she'. Appointing a Co-creator – on a project basis or as a general function in an organization – is the best way to maximize the chances of co-creation success.[3]

> *Co-creation is the glue between functions in an organization, helping them work together in service of their customers' needs."*
> *Paul Thursfield, Service Design Lead, Philips Lighting*

Reading guide for principle 1 – together

One of the questions we encounter the most is: "How do you determine which parties to include in a co-creation trajectory?" Another frequently asked question: "How do you make sure that collaboration between diverse parties will yield useful output?" These questions are central to this chapter:

1. Which parties to involve in complete co-creation?
2. What are the prerequisites for productive collaboration?

1.   Anderson, C. (2010) *TED Curator Chris Anderson on Crowd Accelerated Innovation.* Wired Magazine (issued 27/12/2010). More information can be found on: http://bit.ly/2wX4lN3

2.   Principle 4 (productive) deals with productive collaboration.

3.   Principle 4 (productive) deals with the Co-creator's role and function profile.

As in every chapter, we will start out with the co-created youth information point JIP Noord as an example, and end with three questions for our readers.

Very diverse parties developed and implemented JIP Noord[4]
The case JIP Noord clearly illustrates how comprehensive the collaboration in complete co-creation can be. The list of potential partners that the Co-creator made at the beginning of the trajectory included more than twenty different organizations, such as local high schools, youth work, debt sanity organizations, institutions for health and well-being, and the police. All of these players were involved in the process from the beginning. Other than youth and potential implementation partners, various internal and external experts helped develop JIP Noord. For instance, an architect was hired to design the location, a designer to create a logo and house style, a web designer to create a website, an internal communication expert to write press releases and to make sure that design and contents of all online and offline communication materials stay in line with the city guidelines. None of these experts had experienced co-creation with youth before, yet all indicated to be positively surprised with their input.

1.   Which parties to involve in complete co-creation?

Because the exact list of relevant parties depends on the challenge, the Co-creator will have to tailor-make it. To do so, he will first ponder the why, what, and how of a potential co-creation trajectory:

1. **Why** start a co-creation trajectory? Or: what is the *challenge* at hand?
2. **What** should the co-creation trajectory deliver? Or: what is its *objective*?
3. **How** to solve the challenge? Or: *to co-create or not to co-create*?
4. **Who** needs to solve the challenge? Or: who are *directly* and *indirectly* involved??

Answering these four questions is the starting phase of a complete co-creation trajectory.[5] This phase is often skipped or not carried out thoroughly. That is a pity, because the sharp phrasing of challenge, objective, and method provides clear guidelines, which are necessary for involving the right people, getting them on track, and ultimately – the realization of successful co-creation.

---

4.   Background information on this case can be found in the introduction to this book.

5.   Principle 3 (ongoing) presents an overview of the five phases of Complete Co-creation.

CO-CREATING A REMOTE SERVICE WITH SENIORS[6]

Challenge (why)	Seniors in the Dutch county Geldrop Mierlo prefer aging in the comfort of their own homes over moving into an institution, but they lack awareness of the remote services that are offered for older people living at home.
Objective (what)	Within six months: realize a remote service for seniors that allows them to keep on living in their own homes, and which has an awareness of 75% among the seniors (75+) in the county one year after introduction.
Co-creation or not (how)	Yes: to make the perspective of the seniors and their caretakers leading to the development process of the new service and its marketing, they need to play an active role in it. Moreover, on its way to become more client-oriented, the initiating organization wants to use this co-creation trajectory as a possibility for learning on the job. Thus, all relevant employees will be made available to participate.
Involved parties (who)	Directly involved: care provider Zuidzorg and its PuntExtra service, local seniors and their caretakers (private caretakers as well as professionals such as neighborhood nurses), design research agency STBY, and the Waag Society's Creative Care Lab. Indirectly involved: county Geldrop Mierlo government workers.

SMS ALERT MOLENWIJK: A SUCCESSFUL NEIGHBORHOOD INITIATIVE IN AMSTERDAM-NOORD[7]

Challenge (why)	Reducing vandalism and criminality in order to raise the quality of living among the neighborhood's residents.
Objective (what)	Within a year: shrinking the neighborhood's criminality record with 50% and realizing a significant rise in the perceived safety among the residents.
Co-creation or not (how)	Yes: the initiative was started by the neighborhood's residents as end-users of the neighborhood. Several residents are leading the process, supported by a large group of enthusiasts that are willing to help. Moreover, there are direct contacts with local institutions, supporting the process and willing to participate in it.
Involved parties (who)	Directly involved: a group active Molenwijk residents, an involved city employee, several local police officers and several local store owners. Indirectly involved: all Molenwijk residents (including the local vandals, criminals, and their victims), all local store owners, the local police department, local youth work, and other potential local partners, such as schools, rehabilitation, debt services, security organizations etc.

Why: the challenge

The challenge – the reason for starting a co-creation trajectory – always pertains to a threat or opportunity for the initiating party. Phrasing the challenge in one sentence requires focus and makes for an unequivocal process, in which all participants share the same mission.

CASE 9

Various challenges occurred during the co-creation of JIP Noord

Various challenges occurred during the co-creation of JIP Noord. After the concept JIP Noord had been developed and had to be implemented, the challenges became more specific. Some examples:

- JIP Noord's location needs to offer space to an information store with a warm, yet professional atmosphere, as well as a private space for individual encounters.
- On JIP Noord's website youth need to be able to quickly gather all relevant information and it should also offer direct consultation.
- A stand for school exchange markets needs to clearly show what JIP Noord is and what's in it for youth.

In order to place a challenge on the organizational calendar and create support for it, the Co-creator needs to convincingly show its relevance. A quick research can underscore the challenge's relevance for the initiating organization and the intended end-users.[8]

What: the objective

When the challenge is summarized and its relevance proven, the Co-creator needs to link an objective to it. The objective deals with the relation between challenge and organizational strategy (mission and vision), and answers the question: "What do we want to achieve when?"

Objectives can pertain to anything: from claiming market share to intensifying client loyalty or capitalizing on societal tendencies. Whatever the challenge, a careful definition is necessary to guide the co-creation trajectory. It is important to clarify the duration of

6.   The case as described here serves an illustrative purpose and may not match reality in terms of facts and numbers. More information about this case can be found here: http://bit.ly/2wZ7mtT

7.   The case as described here serves an illustrative purpose and may not match reality in terms of facts and numbers. More information about this case can be found here: http://bit.ly/2vT6Tb5

8.   This would typically be a combination of a desk research and a survey and/or street research. Principle 2 (with end users) deals with these and other research techniques.

the co-creation process and to specify points of evaluation. A proven tool to do this is the SMART-principle. SMART means that the objective be Specific, Measurable, Acceptable, Realistic, and Timely.[9] Usually, a SMART objective is paraphrased in one sentence.

In order to allow enough freedom for the collaborating players to find the optimal solution, it is important to loosely phrase the objective in terms of output. At the same time, enthusiasm for a solution that is absolutely outside of the initiating organization's scope needs to be prevented. That calls for a clear definition of the boundaries within which the solution must be found. For instance, when a co-creation effort needs to yield a marketing campaign, the initiating organization can give the team a budget and positioning statement, such as a Brand Key.[10] Given this budget and brand positioning, the team is free in their choice of marketing tools, channels, content, and tone of voice.

How: co-creation or not

Refraining from starting a co-creation trajectory indicates the existence barriers against complete co-creation. Examples are a lack of time, capacity or budget. Another potential barrier could be a lack of experience – not knowing how to co-create or where and how to find participants.[11] These are legitimate reasons to opt for a different method. They are signals that the organization is not ready for co-creation. Starting a co-creation process anyway is setting out for disappointment.

As a tool to determine whether the organization is ready for co-creation, we present the Complete Co-creation Self-Scan. An organization is only 'co-creation ready' when all questions are answered with YES. When there are NO's or MAYBE's among the answers, this means that more work is needed on that point. In that case it is better to not (yet) start a complete co-creation trajectory, but settle with a different, more familiar approach.

> 99 *We decided not to engage in co-creation (yet), because we realized we weren't prepared for it. We needed to fix that first!"*
> *Marketing Director, Retail*

---

9.   More information on SMART objectives (or comparable) can be found here: Doran, G. T. (1981). "There's a S.M.A.R.T. way to write management's goals and objectives". *Management Review* (AMA FORUM) 70 (11): 35–36 and Yemm, G. (2013). *Essential Guide to Leading Your Team: How to Set Goals, Measure Performance and Reward Talent*. Financial Times Publishing.

10.   A positioning instrument like the Brand Key provides a framework for distinctly positioning a brand in relation to its competitors. More information about the Brand Key can be found here: http://bit.ly/2xyc2tA Apart from the Brand Key there are lots of other brand positioning models around, such as the Keller Brand Equity model: http://bit.ly/2wWMxlo

11.   Principle 6 (supported) deals with barriers against complete co-creation.

The Complete Co-creation Self-Scan

PRINCIPLE	QUESTION
Together	Are all involved internal and external players willing to collaborate, given the challenge and objective?
With end-users	Does the initiating organization know who the end-users are, and does it want to give them a central role during the development process?
Productive	Is there a competent Co-creator with enough time, resources, and decision making power to guide the process from the definition of the challenge until the implementation and tracking of the solution?
Ongoing	Is the initiating organization willing and capable to accept co-creation as an ongoing process, with all relevant parties playing an active role in every phase?
Transparent	Did the involved parties verbalize the intention that they will openly share all information relevant to the challenge at hand (or, preferably, did they sign a contract to do so)?
Supported	Do all relevant parties support complete co-creation as the leading approach and do they accept all of its implications?
Value-driven	Does the initiating organization aspire to create sustainable value on the levels of end-users, organization, and planet?

The question "who are the end-users?" is second in this scan. However, we recommend organizations considering complete co-creation to ask this question first. It is not uncommon to lack a clear idea for whom a potential solution for an identified challenge will be relevant. Organizations may define a wide segment as end-users, for instance "small and medium-sized enterprises" (SME's). That is too wide for a co-creation trajectory. Within the segment SME's are countless sub-segments that have very different needs.

For some of these the challenge may be relevant, for others not at all. Before starting a co-creation trajectory, the organization will have to conduct research in order to find out whether some of the sub-segments recognize the challenge, and for whom a potential solution might be relevant. Only when this group has been clearly defined and the organization knows how to reach them, they can start to co-create.

Who: involved parties

Based on the challenge and objective, the Co-creator will make a list of internal and external, directly and indirectly involved parties. With involved parties we mean *all* parties that are relevant in one way or another for the development and/or implementation of the solution that will be co-created. This list should be longer rather than shorter, since not involving a player that later appears to be of importance, will lead to a sub-optimal outcome.
It is a good idea to divide the list into stakeholders, key players, and end-users.[12] As soon as it is clear how much time the various involved parties want to invest, the co-creation team and advisory council can be formed. Later in the process, in the phase of optimization and implementation, opportunity work groups will be added.

The involved parties in a co-creation process

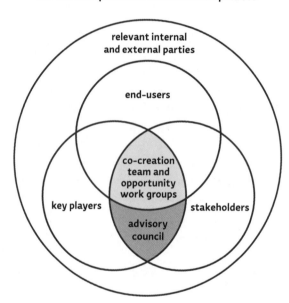

Stakeholders

Stakeholders are decision makers that need to support to co-creation process, but are seldom actively engaging in it. They are usually the management of the initiating organization plus potential investors and partner organizations, possibly also politicians. To maintain stakeholder support, a few update-meetings are usually enough.[13] Of course it is possible that stakeholders feel so involved with the challenge that they want to fulfill a more intensive role as key players or even members of the co-creation team.

Key players

Key players are indirectly involved internal and external players that are important for the co-creation trajectory because of their unique knowledge, experience, or network. The Co-creator keeps them up-to-date throughout the co-creation trajectory, consults them when necessary, and may ask them at specific points in the process to actively co-create. However, they don't structurally participate in the co-creation team.

Internal key players may be: employees that will play a role in the implementation of the solution, employees that have direct contact with end-users, and employees that deal with the organization's marketing and PR. For instance, people working on the departments of communication, marketing, sales, and client services, as well as front desk employees and hostesses. *External* key players are all that may play a role in the production and implementation chain after launching the solution. For instance: suppliers, partner organizations, designers, web designers, and retailers.

The co-creation team

The co-creation team is a multi-disciplinary group of people that carries out the co-creation trajectory. The Co-creator guides this team, which consists of representatives of the initiating organization, end-users, and several key players. Stakeholders may also take a seat in this team.

The co-creation team is the core team, which may be expanded with relevant key players in several phases of the co-creation trajectory. Asking attendees of a large kick-off event (where end-users were invited to as well) to actively participate in the co-creation trajectory will yield a list of interested people.[14] The Co-creator may be able to assemble a co-creation team solely based on this list. If not, he may have to proactively approach certain players of his original list. Which people will end up in the co-creation team ultimately depends on potential participants' motivation and availability.

In order to be flexible, yet diverse, the ideal size for a co-creation team is eight people. During the complete co-creation trajectory, this team will meet regularly to discuss progress, analyze preliminary outcomes, develop solutions, determine next steps, and decide which players to involve in which step.

The team's diverse participants' input will vary along the process in terms of intensity and frequency, according to their specific strengths. For instance, conceptual thinkers will play a relatively large role during the first phases of research and concept development, whereas the practical, action-driven types will leave their mark more on the phase of implementation.

12. In the introduction of this book we defined the term 'end users' as follows: end-users are the (intended) target group of the solution to be co-created: the people for whom the solution needs to be relevant and attractive to use.

13. Principle 6 (supported) deals with the creation and maintenance of support.

14. Principle 3 (ongoing) deals with the kick-off session.

An ever changing co-creation team guided the development of JIP Noord [15]

The co-creation team that guided the development of JIP Noord changed size and make-up throughout the development process. Still, there was a fixed core of 'die-hards', consisting of the external Co-creator, the manager of the Parent & Child Center Amsterdam-Noord [16], the policy advisor Youth & Family, the policy advisor Youth 12+, a junior policy advisor (who was detached as JIP Noord employee after launch and later became JIP Noord's manager), a managers and a youth worker of the local youth work organization DOCK, a manager and an employee of the welfare organization Spirit, a youth worker of Streetcornerwork, and four local youth.

End-users in the co-creation team

In order to realize the optimal solution, it is important that the co-creation team exists of players that will influence the performance of the solution after launch. It seems obvious that the intended end-users should be among them! Chances that the solution will be of real value for them will increase dramatically when end-user perspective is leading throughout the development process. [17]

This may sound like an open door, but the reality is that project managers often choose to stay within the comfortable walls of their own organization. This way, everyone's role is clear up front, and meetings are simply planned in the internal calendar. Such processes are often referred to as co-creation, because a group of people created something together. However, since end-users and other relevant parties were not added, this is *incomplete* co-creation at best.

Another possibility is that end-users do actively participate, but that some important groups were left out – with a sub-optimal solution as the result. This regularly happens in the development of products for children. Often, these are either tailor-made to the kids' needs and wishes, overlooking the parents' perspective. Those are the types of products that children nag about, but parents hate to spend their money on. The opposite happens, too, resulting in products that parents like to buy, but get neglected by their children.

15. This case was introduced in the introduction of this book.

16. During the period that JIP Noord was developed, Amsterdam had so-called "OKC's": Parent and Child Centers. In the rest of The Netherlands these centers were referred to as "CJG's" (Centers for Youth and Family). Nowadays, Amsterdam has mobile "OKT's" (Parent and Child Teams).

17. Principle 2 (with end-users) deals with where to find and how to motivate end-users to participate in complete co-creation"

Online job-platform developed in co-creation with one of two user groups

Following the success of online platform Peerby, which enables neighborhood residents to borrow each other's stuff, a large publisher developed a conceptual platform that allowed youth to post jobs that they could do for their neighbors. Think walking the dog, mowing the lawn, washing the car, or watching the kids. Because the concept was developed in co-creation with youth it matched their needs and wishes in terms of look and feel, as well as functionalities and usability.

When the beta-version was launched in a Dutch neighborhood, this quickly became popular among the local youth. Lots of jobs were published online, but the intended customers remained passive. Were adult residents of the neighborhood able to find the platform at all? Or was it somehow not attractive to them? In order to check existing hypotheses about the drivers and barriers of the group potential grown-up customers, the publisher organized a session with several involved employees, the platform designer, and a group of potential customers within the age range of 30 through 60 years. This revealed several barriers regarding quality control, safety, and usability. Had the group potential customers been involved in the co-creation trajectory right from the start, this 'loop' back into concept development would have been prevented.

Other relevant parties in the co-creation team

Failing to add end-users to a development process is a pitfall that should be prevented – that much is clear. At the same time, other relevant parties should not be overlooked either. When the initiating organization involves plenty of end-users, but no other relevant parties, it is not co-creating, but conducting market research.[18]

Diversity as a formative principle for the co-creation team

In assembling the co-creation team, diversity is an important aspect. Diversity – as in background, age, lifestyle, experience, expertise etc. – stimulates out-of-the-box thinking.[19] Moreover, diversity increases the likelihood that all puzzle pieces necessary for an optimal solution will be brought to the table. Despite the proven advantages of diversity, the pitfall to involve only similar people in the co-creation team is big. People tend to feel more comfortable in a homogenous setting, and this is also less work to organize.

18.   Principle 2 (with end-users) discusses conducting market research instead of co-creation.

19.   More information about the importance of diversity in innovation can be found here: Phillips, K. (2014). *How Diversity Makes Us Smarter: Being around people who are different from us makes us more creative, more diligent and harder- working.* Scientific American. And here: http://bit.ly/2h0Aahr

Opportunity work groups

During the co-creation trajectory, opportunity work groups will arise. These groups will work together on specific themes, such as packaging, design, social media, website, or location styling. Opportunity work groups consist of various internal and external players, among them end-users and experts that are relevant for the work group's theme. Depending on the theme, these could be architects, web designers, stylists, communication experts, etc.[20]

Advisory council

It is a good idea to found a multi-disciplinary advisory council at the start of the co-creation trajectory. This group consists of stakeholders and key players that don't take place in the co-creation team, but whose sympathy and support are crucial for the trajectory's success. They get together every once in a while, for a quick process update and a brain dump, during which the group is encouraged to share their ideas and advice.[21]

2. What are the prerequisites for productive collaboration?

We identify five prerequisites for the productive collaboration between various parties: equality, transparency, co-ordination, continuity, and motivation. Each of these prerequisites comes with a specific pitfall. A competent Co-creator will always stay on the lookout for these pitfalls.

Equality

Equality in the interrelationships of all participants is a defining characteristic of a productive co-creation culture. It means that the co-creating players – as different as they might be – respect each other, give each other space, and respond in a constructive way to each other's input. Each participant feels involved, appreciated, and stimulated. They are aware of the fact that every single one of them holds a unique piece of a puzzle that can only be completed by working together.

Creating an atmosphere of equality in a co-creation process requires a strong social antenna and good group management skills. The same is true for maintaining a creative mood by avoiding 'idea killers' and catalyzing out-of-the-box thinking. Thus, especially during physical meetings with diverse parties, a competent process manager is crucial.[22] This can be the Co-creator, but it can also be a professional moderator, trained in creativity-stimulating techniques.

20. Principle 3 (ongoing) deals with the role and make-up parallel work groups.

21. Principle 6 (supported) deals with the support-enhancing effects of a multi-disciplinary advisory group.

22. More information about idea killers can be found here: http://www.ideakillers.net/.

LEGO SERIOUS PLAY® uses LEGO® as a metaphor in solving challenges

LEGO® SERIOUS PLAY® (LSP) is a method that can only be applied by certified LEGO® SERIOUS PLAY® facilitators. Participants use fictitious scenarios and LEGO®-constructions to develop new ideas, strategies, and concepts. The method can be integrated within a complete co-creation process. LEGO® SERIOUS PLAY® was developed in the nineties by Johan Roos and Bart Victor (at that time professors at the IMD Business School), Robert Rasmussen (at that time director product development for the educative market at LEGO®), and Dave Owens, professor at the Vanderbilt University. Certified LSP facilitator Patrizia Bertini explains in an interview with TheCoCreators: "LEGO® blocks function as mediators between participants and help break through potential hierarchies and power play that can often sabotage creative processes." According to Patrizia roughly 70 to 80% of our brain cells are in contact with our hands. "That means that by using LEGO® blocks, neural connections are activated that stimulate creativity among participants." Patrizia mentions the Global GovJam 2013 in Bologna as an example of a successful LSP workshop.[23] Global GovJam organizes events at which partipants have 48 hours to develop solutions for challenges in the public sector. "In Bologna I moderated an LSP workshop in which fifteen very different people participated: from government workers to students and from researchers to local politicians. The theme was: 'Hic Sunt Dragones' (Latin for 'these are the dragons')." During the first part of the workshop, the group of reflected on these dragons: unexpected, negative aspects of the local government. "Each participant used LEGO® blocks to create a unique landscape around this theme. Then the group discussed these metaphors, which helped to reach a shared understanding of the dragons around several themes."

The next step was to develop solutions. "First, each participant created his or her own personal response in the form of a LEGO® model. This gave rise to a constructive negotiation process, with participants sharing stories and researching each other's models to develop a shared solution. In the end, the whole group was happy with both the result and the process: a positive debate between civilians and government workers. The workshop yielded two concrete concepts, which the group optimized during the second day."

Equality in the interaction does not automatically make all participants equal owners of the co-created solution. In most cases, the initiating organization is the owner of the solution and any other output. Before starting the creative process, it is a good idea to have the co-creation team sign a contract which legally defines ownership and holds participants to secrecy during the process.

23.   More information on Global GovJam can be found here: www.govjam.org.

The filling in reflex

Handing over process control to a group and reducing one's own input to that of an equal group member takes modesty, openness, and empathy. A lack of any these can feed the 'filling in reflex', where a dominant player determines the input of the other participants. We call it a reflex because it is usually a dominant player's automatic response and not a consciously planned process.

Filling in may take the form of an overpowering attitude, suggestive questions, and limiting assignments, or even a direct devaluation of any input that does not support one's own ideas. When this happens, the puzzle principle cannot unfold because the dominant player is, quite literally, silencing the others. Research shows that successful teams allow every team member the same amount of 'speaking time', which adds to a higher collective IQ of the group.[24] Contrastingly, a team's collective IQ is lowered when some team members are talking structurally more than others.

CASE 13

"Co-creation" with parents by a knowledge institute

A knowledge institute wanted to co-create with parents as 'end-users of the knowledge on childhood development' that the institute continuously gathers and spreads. A moderator was hired to lead a brainstorm session dealing with the question what kind of knowledge parents need about their growing children, and how the institute can best fill in this need.

Several of the institute's employees had already worked on a few concept starters with respect to the institute's potential relation to parents. Together with some parents, these employees participated in the brainstorm. Prior to the session, they explicitly briefed the moderator to work towards one of these concept starters as the outcome. Even if the moderator had wanted to comply, she was never really in control of the session flow. This was because right off the bat the institute's CEO took on the role of session leader. He kicked off with a long introduction about his institute's intermediary function between knowledge about children's development and parents as educators. He then asked his staff what they thought the institute had to offer. Each of them held a lengthy exposé about the benefits of the institute as objective information provider. By the time it was the parents' turn to react, they only dared agree with the prior speakers. Finally, one of the employees presented the concept starters. Explicitly seeking eye contact with just his own employees, the CEO invited all participants to react. Although the moderator tried to entice the parents to share their own perceptions and ideas, they just quietly looked at the CEO and agreed with the opinion of the staff. After the session the CEO scolded the moderator for not making the parents come up with refreshing and novel ideas. "But they may very well not have been able to be novel and refreshing anyway," he concluded. "We really tried that co-creation stuff, but clearly it doesn't work. Next time we'll just develop our own ideas again; this was a waste of time."

Dominance

Bringing the puzzle principle into practice can be hard, especially if there is a history of hierarchy between the collaborating players. A huge pitfall is for the initiating or largest organization to take on a dominant stance, failing to allow the other players the space they need to give their best input. In response they may resort to either submission or rebellion. *Submission* means that the other players will not speak their truth, with the dominant player unilaterally dictating the process and its output. Best case scenario is that the outcome will be similar to what would have been delivered by an internal process. When *rebellion* occurs, there will be no usable output at all, since the other players will actively oppose the collaboration, or passively sabotage it.

Apart from not leading to optimal process output, dominance of one of the players also means a frustrating experience for the others – something that should be prevented at all times. Research shows that one negative experience spreads faster than several positive ones.[25] The other players may refrain from further collaboration, or even spread negativity about the dominant player. Ultimately, this may lead to end-users' disloyalty.

Transparency

Only when the collaborating players are open with respect to anything pertaining to the challenge and its solution, complete co-creation can occur.[26] Keeping relevant information from the other players will lead to a sub-optimal outcome of the development process. It may also evoke feelings of insecurity, frustration, and powerlessness among the other players. Worst case scenario is a breach of trust, resulting in stagnation of the collaboration, and possibly broadcasting negativity about the initiating organization.

Co-ordination

Although a creative process needs a certain extent of freedom, this does not mean that it should be chaotic. Process co-ordination is essential to keep the collaborating players focused and motivated. While allowing regular diverging to stimulate out-of-the-box creativity, the Co-creator will eventually lead the process with logical steps to a concrete solution for the pre-determined challenge. This can be a product, service, experience, brand, marketing tool, strategy, scenario, or even a new organization.

24. More information on the functioning of teams and the variable 'equality in distribution of conversational turn-taking' can be found here: http://nyti.ms/2h3JwVY

25. More about the effects of a negative experience can be found here: *Customer Service and Business Results: a Survey of Customer Service from mid-size Companies* (april 2013), a research that was carried out by Dimensional Research and sponsored by Zendesk: http://bit.ly/2xZk3UI. The entire article can be found here: Baumeister, R., Bratslavsky, E., Finkenauer, C. & Vohs, K. (2001). *Bad Is Stronger Than Good.* Review of General Psychology 2001. Vol. 5. No. 4. 323-370. Zie ook: http://bit.ly/2vTlp2w

Effective co-ordination needs a competent Co-creator. The collaborating players must feel free to play around on their brain waves, not hindered by practical issues regarding the development process. A good Co-creator knows how to stimulate creativity (divergence), when and how to cluster the creative outbursts into concept platforms (convergence), and what next steps to take (implementation).[27]

A lack of structure is the result of not appointing a Co-creator at all, or appointing an incompetent one. In an unstructured process, the creative process may not flow at all, or it may yield an abundance of loose ideas that are not taken to the next stage. Thus, an unstructured process not only leads to unusable output, but also to unmotivated participants. It is very frustrating to share great ideas, only to see them strand. Therefore, participants will sooner or later leave when the collaboration remains chaotic.

Continuity

Continuity refers to collaboration over an extended period of time, as opposed to a temporary project. In complete co-creation, the initiating organization, end-users, and other relevant parties agree to collaborate for an *unspecified* period of time – at least until a promising solution has been found and implemented. After launching the solution, during the phases of implementation and tracking, the various parties should at least stay passively involved as sparring partners. Ideally, they actively share responsibility as co-implementors or even co-owners.

> 66 *The more the customer is involved in the process of service production and delivery, the greater the perceived value and satisfaction. […] Consumers (as individuals and as a group of interacting subjects) become partial employees and employees become partial consumers."* Cova, B. Professor of Marketing at Kedge Business School and Dalli, D. Professor of Marketing at University of Pisa[28]

For longer-term involvement to occur, all parties need to feel safe and not be afraid that the collaboration will suddenly be halted. That means that end-users and other relevant parties should fulfill a structural role within the initiating organization, which should always be open to their input. There are several ways in which collaborating parties can be continuously involved in an organization's challenges, for instance by means of an online community (self-built or pre-existing), as an advisory board or perhaps an ambassadors club.[29]

---

26. In this chapter we only briefly discuss transparency as a prerequisite for productive collaboration. Principle 5 (transparent) deals with transparency in more detail.

Continuous collaboration with end-users helped Gynzy make the digiboard more relevant[30]

Gynzy, founded in 2009, develops online software for digital school boards. Rutger Peters, co-founder and Company Dean, in an interview with TheCoCreators: "We came from the online casual gaming world and wanted to use our knowledge and experience to aid the digitization of primary education. Because we didn't know anything about education, our first step was to seek direct contact with teachers, children, and their parents, as well as school principals and education experts.

Quickly, we noticed that digiboards had successfully taken over the old-fashioned blackboards, but were hardly ever used to their full potential. We decided to make it our mission to drastically simplify digiboard use and make relevant content readily accessible. It took four months of intense immersion in the world of teachers and children to really grasp the needs. Because we took so much time to do this, the development phase was a breeze. On January first, 2010, we started programming, and half March we had a running prototype. A group of 1000 teachers actively worked with the prototype between March and the summer vacation. We spent hours in classrooms observing, and we integrated large feedback buttons in the prototype, which generated a continuous stream of points for improvement. Thus, we were able to realize a perfect fit between the software and teacher needs. This approach also yielded new ideas for digital content. For instance, teachers asked us to develop something to put pupils in the spotlight on their birthday. We built a fun application which had children blow out virtual candles on a birthday cake. That is now our most popular app! Around thirty percent of our digiboard software is filled in with stuff like that, which is not related to the formal lessons. The continuous collaboration with teachers allowed us to take the optimized product to market in September 2010, our year of introduction. Three years later, with more than half of all Dutch primary school teachers already using our software, we launched in the United States.

We keep developing – co-creation never stops. The feedback keeps streaming and everyone within Gynzy knows that we can only get better by reaching out and collaborating with our end-users and others. This approach is much appreciated by our customers. Teachers sometimes tell us that it is the first time in their career that someone really listens to them and actually does something with their ideas. A wonderful example is a teacher who approached me at an exchange market, and said: "I am one of the founders of Gynzy!" She turned out to be one of our first users. Fantastic!"

27. In this chapter we only introduce the Co-creator's co-ordinating role as a prerequisite for productive collaboration. Principle 4 (productive) deals with the role of the Co-creator.

28. Cova, B. & Dalli, D. (2009) *Working Consumers: The next Step in marketing Theory*. Marketing Theory 9(3), p319 Principle 2 (with end-users) deals with the involvement of end-users in complete co-creation.

29. Principle 2 (with end-users) deals with the involvement of end-users in complete co-creation.

30. More information about Gynzy can be found here: www.gynzy.nl and here: www.gynzy.com .

Gynzy's teacher community for sharing and discussing ideas

I suggest you ...

Click here to start sharing your idea

Hot   Top   New   Category   ▾   Status   ▾   My feedback

12
votes

Vote

I teach students with significant special needs. I need to be able to create my own boards (e.g. memory, sentence builders, graphs, question

I teach students with significant special needs. I need to be able to create my own boards (e.g. memory, sentence builders, graphs, question of the day, etc.) using pictures specific to my required curriculum. I found a memory board for your own content but it doesn't let you use pictures. Please consider adding activities that would allow us to use pictures instead of words, letters, numbers, or sentences.

OPEN FOR VOTING · 0 comments · Activity ideas · Flag idea as inappropriate…

48
votes

Vote

Reading skills and famous people

I think more literary material and historical figures would help round things out. My students need a lot of help with reading skills.

9 comments · Instruction* · Flag idea as inappropriate…

Co-creation as an experiment

Many organizations perceive co-creation as an experiment or temporary project. When the intended outcome has been manifested, the collaboration is aborted. Although limited pilot projects can be necessary to introduce the benefits of co-creation into an organization, it is best to not linger in project thinking. Co-creation only leads to value creation when all players embrace it as a shared way of thinking and doing, which has no beginning and no end. In other words: complete co-creation is never an experiment, but always a *structural* approach of reality.

CASE 15

Limited collaboration within a large government institution resulted in disappointment

A process manager within a large government-related organization shared his experiences with limited collaboration in an interview with TheCoCreators: "For an organizational innovation trajectory we identified a latent need of the target group youth and young adults. I got the opportunity to find a solution in co-creation with this target group – an entirely new approach for our organization. Some colleagues were enthusiastic about it; others skeptical. Personally, I was convinced right of the bat that this approach would yield a concrete solution with real value for the intended end-users.

We gathered a group of youth for a few brainstorm sessions, during which they developed their ideas and presented these to stakeholders. The process yielded very diverse concepts, much further developed than I had expected. In this phase, I was in a flow and saw lots of opportunities for implementation, but unfortunately the organization was not ready to commit. The ideas were too far out of the box and the management dismissed them as unrealistic. The process was abandoned as an unsuccessful innovation experiment and never had a follow-up.

Afterwards I felt exhausted and disappointed, not taken serious by the management. The involved youth were disappointed, too, and broke contact with the organization – such a shame, because there were real talents among them who could have been of great value.

Evaluating, I think that I was seriously lacking support, as well as freedom. Everything had to happen according to tight organizational guidelines, and failing was not an option. Moreover, the internal knowledge specialists that I wanted to involve didn't want to commit. I had no means to break through the organizational paradigms and more than once, I hade to ignore the rules in order to proceed. I also inadvertently got mixed up in power play between departments, and felt continuously alert. I learned the hard way that time, commitment from all involved players, and a safe experimentation space are very important if you want to start co-creating in a large, established organization. In hindsight, none of these prerequisites was fulfilled."

Risks of halting co-creation

Halting or aborting a co-creation process comes with three risks.

1. Involved players break contact with the initiating organization

Involving end-users and other relevant parties creates expectations. Even if they are officially outsiders, they feel valued and taken serious because they are part of an important process. Typically, they will find their own input relevant and will expect action resulting from it. Based on their invested time and energy, they will expect to stay involved – or at least receive regular updates. When this does not happen, they may no longer feel part of the process and may cut the relationship with the initiating organization.

> 66 *If you go out and say to people you want to involve them and then you don't act up on it, you begin to lose credibility very quickly. [...] In a community you are asking for people's time and contribution. What they expect in return is for things to be better and you therefore have to be able to prove that what they have said made a difference."*
> *Rick Jenner, Head of New Product Development Insight, Virgin Media*[31]

31. From: Ind, N., Fuller, C., Trevail, C. (2012). Brand *Together: How Co-Creation Generates Innovation and Re-energizes Brands.* Kogan Page Limited. London

When involved parties break contact with the initiating organization, the latter will have to find new collaboration partners for future co-creation efforts – a rather inefficient process.

2. Involved players spread negativity about the initiating organization

Simply pulling the plug from the collaboration, without announcing or explaining this to the involved parties, will most likely result in delusion and rebellion. Even if the initiating organization does indicate to abort further collaboration with a plausible explanation, participants that were collaborating enthusiastically before, may break contact. They may feel revengeful for being 'used'. This will surely give rise to negative talk or active sabotage.

CASE 16

Henkel disppointed end-users

In 2011 Henkel launched a crowdsource, asking German users of their dish washing liquid Pril to develop a packaging design. This yielded more than 50.000 responses, such as designs with butterflies and flower fields, but also absurd concepts, like a chicken-design with the one-liner "tastes like chicken!", a monster face, a sausage, and a nose wearing glasses.

Henkel asked consumers to vote; the design with the most votes would be printed on real Pril packaging. However, that turned out to be the chicken design, which didn't correspond one bit with Pril's brand values. Henkel then decided to change the rules and have a jury choose the winning design.

The public responded with frustration, overflowing Pril's Facebook feed with responses such as 'ridiculous', 'horrible', and 'terrible ending'. Proper communication could have prevented this. If the crowdsource assignment had contained Pril's brand values as prerequisites for the designs, it probably would not have been necessary to adapt the rules. If, however, Henkel would have still seen a need for different rules, honest and unequivocal communication of the reasons would have been enough to prevent most negative reactions.[32]

3. The initiating organization falls back to internal processes

During a flirt with co-creation, the initiating organization may realize consciously or subconsciously that complete co-creation implies a fundamentally different way of working. When the organization is not ready for that, it will return to trusted development processes, using arguments like: 'co-creation takes too much time', 'co-creation just doesn't suit us', or 'co-creation doesn't deliver'.

32.   More information about the Pril case can be found here: http://bit.ly/2h1VAHk

Falling back to internal processes means that the organization will not be able to optimally benefit from co-creation, and ultimately will find itself surpassed by competitors that do use structural co-creation in order to realize a higher relevance for end-users.

Motivation

When participants only collaborate because they are forced to or will receive a certain reward, the co-creation process is unlikely to lead to the best outcome. In order to realize the positive atmosphere necessary for finding and developing the optimal solution, all participants need to be intrinsically motivated. For that, the Co-creator is the key.[33]

Intrinsic motivation among members of a multidisciplinary co-creation team only develops when they, despite differences, feel connected with one another. A certain amount of team building is necessary in order to create a shared experience of relevance and urgency – the idea to work together on something useful.[34]

This does not mean that extrinsic motivational means like rewards are not done. On the contrary, there are instances in which these can be very useful or even necessary to entice people to start collaborating or to re-energize collaborating players.[35] This is particularly true for participants who do not have a direct stake in the solution at hand and who make money selling their time.[36] Whether such people are participating or not, a shared mission is essential, motivational elements in the co-creation process are important, and teambuilding is a priority for any co-creation effort.

3. Questions to our readers

1. Do you know a competent Co-creator within your organization?
a. If so, why do you think this person is competent as a Co-creator?
b. If not, where do you think a competent Co-creator might be found outside of your organization?

2. Do you think your organization can fulfill all prerequisites for complete co-creation? If not, which of the prerequisites need to be dealt with first, and how?

3. Which parties would you involve in a co-creation process – given the most important challenge your organization is facing right now?

---

33. Principle 4 (productive) deals with the co-ordinating and motivating role of the Co-creator.

34. Principle 6 (supported) deals with intrinsic motivation as prerequisite for successful co-creation.

35. Principe 2 (with end-users) deals with incentives.

36. Principe 6 (supported) deals with rewarding external parties.

Principle 1: Together.
Complete co-creation is based on equal
collaboration between all relevant
internal and external parties.

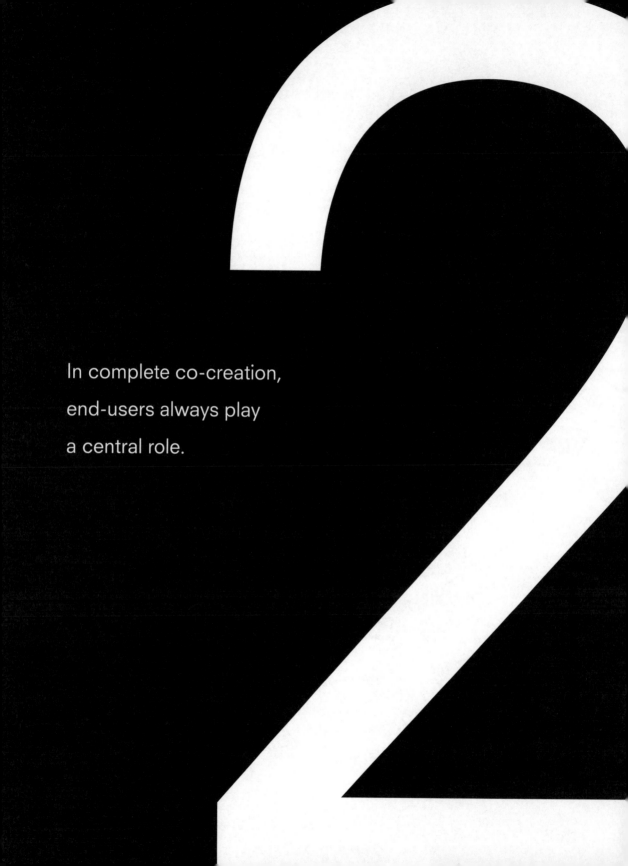

In complete co-creation,
end-users always play
a central role.

PRINCIPLE 2
WITH END-USERS

Over the past decades, the realization that real value only emerges from end-users' needs has caused a shift from a product-driven to a client-centered approach. This has happened among large marketing organizations, as well as government organizations, NGO's, SME's,[1] and business-to-business organizations. Although the notion that end-users are important has been well established, the translation to everyday practice often comes with difficulties.

How does one become client-driven in real life? Surely, *not* by just talking a lot about clients, customers, consumers, citizens, end-users, or target groups. Talking about them is something else than giving them a central position. The latter means giving them a clear voice in the organization – at least when it comes to challenges which affect them directly or indirectly.

> ❝ *It may seem heresy to say so but you don't want to be customer-focused; you want to co-create with your customer. You don't want to be customer-centric; you want to co-innovate with your customer, engage them and build a very different future."*
> Don Tapscott, Canadian entrepreneur, consultant, and speaker[2]

For organizations with loyal fans, the involvement of end-users in co-creation is relatively easy. Fans usually want to help, simply because they are honored that their favorite organization is taking them seriously.

CASE 17

LEGO maintains a continuous dialogue with its fans

During a 2005 user-convention in the United States, LEGO CEO Jørgen Vig Knudstorp said: *"We think innovation will come from a dialogue with the community."*[3] That was the starting point of a continuous dialogue between LEGO and LEGO fans – children and adults alike – in which several online and offline platforms are used to collaboritively identify and solve challenges. For instance, the portal ideas.lego.com allows anyone to upload or visualize ideas.[4] Ideas that generate 10.000 (or more) supporters may be developed into an official LEGO product, in which case the idea-owner receives 1% of the total net revenue. Revenue share is not the most important driver for client participation, though. Even without any incentive, LEGO fans are willing to contribute.[5] Worldwide exist various online and offline communities, founded and managed by LEGO users – from forums to exchange building tips to collectors clubs, to building workshops. These communities are followed closely by LEGO, even though they are not officially related to the organization. LEGO supports its fan clubs with means and knowledge, and contacts them regularly for online and offline collaboration. While LEGO was making loss around the turn of the century, since the start of the co-creative approach revenues and profit have grown explosively, with revenue increasing from around 2.5 billion Euros in 2011 to almost five billion in 2015, and a net profit of around 0.5 billion in 2011 and well over a billion in 2015.[6]

---

1.   The abbreviation SME's stands for: small and medium-sized enterprises.

2.   He said this during the Fujitsu Forum 2017 in Tokyo: http://bit.ly/2y16Aff. More information on Don Tapscott can be found here: htttp://www.dontapscott.com/

Most organizations don't (yet) have loyal fans that spontaneously organize themselves to tackle their challenges. That means they will have to actively seek and invite (potential) end-users to work with them. Not knowing who the end-users are, where to find them, and how to motivate them can be reasons to abandon the intention to co-create. Even when they do have loyal fans, organizations may be hesitant to embark on a co-creation adventure, possibly because they are lacking relevant knowledge and experience, or because decision makers are not convinced of the benefits.

Reading guide principle 2 – with end-users

Entirely dedicated to the end-users as essential participants in complete co-creation, this chapter seeks answers to the following questions:

1. Why would organizations give end-users an active role?
2. What does active end-user involvement look like?
3. How to find, activate, and reward end-users?
4. Can other methods replace end-user involvement?

When reading this chapter, bear in mind that its focus is involving *end-users* in complete co-creation. This does not mean that other players are not important! All relevant parties should be actively involved, as described in other chapters.[7] As usual, we start this chapter with the multi-faceted case JIP Noord as an example and end with three questions to our readers.

CASE 18

Youth as end-users central to JIP Noord's development[8]

The city county Amsterdam-Noord could have found an easier way to comply with the law and establish a local information and advisory service for youth. For instance, for a small fee they could have leased the website of the nation-wide JIP-club. However, that would oppose the objective to create real value and relevance for local youth as end-users. They dismissed the nation-wide JIP-website as amateur-looking, cluttered, containing too much non-relevant information and click-throughs to general, non-valid websites such as Wikipedia. They also stressed that a website alone would never effectively reach them. The city county decided to develop a website for JIP Noord (www.jipnoord.nl) as well as to establish a physical information point in the new school at a stop of the new metro line to Amsterdam-Noord. The relevance of JIP Noord can be inferred from its popularity, not only among local youth, but also youth from other quarters, and even other towns.

3. Antorini, Y. & Muñiz, Jr. M. & Askildsen, T. (2012). *Collaborating With Customer Communities: Lessons From the Lego Group*. MIT Sloan Management Review (Issue: Spring 2012).

4. More information about the LEGO case can be found here: https://ideas.lego.com/ and https://lego.build/2f9jmEo

❝ *This site is too distracting. Too many colors, not clearly organized."*
Busra, 16 years old, co-developer JIP Noord, commenting on the nation-wide JIP site

"To talk to a person is better than to a computer."
Joey, 19 years old, co-developer JIP Noord

"If you want to do something for youth, you have to get to know them.
You need to approach them personally, preferably in their own surroundings."
Omerfaruk, 16 years old, co-developer JIP Noord

"You should have us build the website; then you can be sure that it will be really
interesting for people our age."
Moreyo, 16 years old, co-developer JIP Noord

1.   Why would organizations give end-users an active role?

Giving end-users a central role in taking on challenges leads to recognizable and relevant solutions – a prerequisite for the emergence of loyal fans. Loyal fans may not only give spontaneous tips for the improvement of 'their' organization's products, services or communication, but may also actively engage in the most effective form of advertising: word-of-mouth.[9]

Only customer connected organizations are able to develop and sustain loyal fans. These organizations maintain continuous 'customer connection': they keep contact with their end-users via multiple channels. Thus, these organizations develop 'target group gutfeel': an intuitive understanding of their (intended) end-users' deeper motivations. This allows them to identify unmet needs faster than their competitors, and fill in these needs more efficiently. Moreover, in translating needs to implications, they hardly ever make mistakes. A growing body of evidence shows that gutfeel is often right.[10]

5.   N. Franke and S. Shah. (2003). *How Communities Support Innovative Activities: An Exploration of Assistance and Sharing Among End-users.* Research Policy 32, no.1: 157-78.

6.   From Lego's Group Annual report 2015. http://lego.build/2wYyiMF

7.   Principle 1 (together) explicitly deals with involving all relevant parties in a co-creation trajectory, not just end-users.

8.   The case JIP Noord – including popularity numbers – has been introduced in the introduction of this book.

9.   More information on the power of word of mouth can be found here: http://bit.ly/2xAYwW3

10. More information on the power of gutfeel can be found here: http://bit.ly/2wYUTsv

Target group gut inspires leads IKEA[11]

Every year, IKEA carries out thousands of home visits in different countries to observe people's daily routines, gain understanding of how and why they organize their homes the way they do and anything that frustrates them about their space. Answers and images are then recorded on a vast database.

This is how IKEA feeds its target group gut feel about living in general, as well as its understanding of regional living habits. This can lead to country-specific furniture, such as a Korea-only supersized single bed for small bedrooms. Moreover, target group gut feel determines in-store displays, which have different accents in every country.

The implications of IKEA's continuous target group research are shared through two annual reports: The Curiosity Report, which describes next year's design focus and the Life at Home report, a global study into a particular aspect of home life such as morning rituals or habits around food.

> To make better, more relevant products, we have to be constantly curious about people and their everyday lives: how do they behave, why do they behave like that, and why contemporary phenomena arise."
> Mikael Ydholm, Communication and Innovation Strategist at Inter IKEA

Customer connection as the basis for hypotheses formation

Customer connected organizations seek frequent contact with end-users, rather than mostly talk about them. This does not mean that talking about end-users is wrong. On the contrary, it is a good habit, which should be thought of as forming hypotheses. "Look at this website, no one will be able to navigate properly on it." "Look, this video clip will be a sure hit among youngsters!" These are examples of hypotheses about end-user response.

> I could never have predicted the things these children said... Most striking to me was that all of us expected them to have lost interest in reading anymore, and only want to stare at screens, whereas they themselves said they feel they are gaming too much and want to read more!
> employee of a publisher after group sessions with elementary school children

11.   More information on the IKEA case can be found here: http://bit.ly/2wZ8u34, http://nyti.ms/2fl54h7, http://indy.st/2wbx9lj and here: http://bit.ly/2x3MvHa

Forming hypotheses helps identify gaps in target group understanding and stimulates focus in a development process. However, hypotheses should never be confused with understandings!

Startup Devver mistook unverified hypotheses for understanding

75% of all American startups supported by venture capital fail.[12] A frequent reason for this is that entrepreneurs and investors usually want to take large steps quickly, before verifying the assumptions of the business model. Instead of creating relevance for their (potential) customers, they take crucial decisions purely based on their own experience and know-how. Devver is an example of this. In 2008 Devver started offering cloud-based services for software developers, which would replace traditional desktop tools. Two years later, Devver and its service ceased to exist.
In hindsight founders Benjamin Brinckerhoff and Dan Mayer cite a lack of customer connection as the most important cause of their failing. Minimizing user and buyer contact, they focused on building tools. Had Devver launched a minimal viable product (MVP) or beta-version in an early phase, the company could have co-created its services with end-users so as to ensure relevance and usability.[13] At the same time, first buyers' and users' reactions could have helped installing the necessary gutfeel for successful market launch, such as understanding of price perception and guidelines for communication.[14]

> " We should have focused more on customer development and finding a minimum viable product. [...] But we knew how great [a tool] it was and we felt that time spent talking to customers was time we could be hacking!"
> Benjamin Brinckerhoff, Co-founder Devver

Organizations may base decisions on unverified hypotheses: a website gets a make-over, a video clip is widely spread through media that are popular with youth as the intended target group. This is a dangerous habit, since hypotheses may not be right at all or perhaps just for part of the intended end-users. Thus, the website may lose its normal visitors, and youth may abandon the brand broadcasting that 'silly video clip'.

12.   This number is based on research among 2000 enterprises receiving venture capital between 2004 and 2010. More information on this research by Shikhar Ghosh, senior lecturer at the Harvard Business School, can be found here: http://on.wsj.com/2jrr6Da

13.   An explanation of the terms 'beta-version' and 'MVP' can be found later in this chapater.

14.   More information about the Devver case can be found here: http://bit.ly/2wYbhcG and here: http://hbs.me/2y1jc5Q

> **❝** *After my colleagues create something new - an assignment for an education method or an illustration for example - they often ask me what I think of it. My answer is always that it is irrelevant what I think, but that they have to check with the teachers and students who will have to work with it."*
>
> Ron Huntley, team leader co-creation at Blink

In order to prevent wrong decisions from happening, it is important to always check hypotheses with end-users, possibly further supported by factual information. Hypotheses can be formed in any phase of a development process – consciously or unconsciously. That is why it is important to maintain *continuous* contact with end-users and other relevant players.Should this appear to cause delays, just realize that it is essential for the development of a solution that really serves end-users' needs. Moreover, a hypotheses check doesn't have to take a bunch of time, especially when an organization has its own online platform or social media group.

Customer connection as the basis for customer insight

A customer insight is a deep understanding of end-users' drivers and barriers to display certain behavior. Customer insights follow from endless amounts of data and observations about end-users, fed by continuous customer connection. While rough data easily becomes a chaotic, overwhelming information swamp that is useful to no-one, customer insight will guide the co-creation trajectory to a recognizable and attractive solution.[15]

> **❝** *With our business becoming digital and connected to the internet, so too our ways of innovating are shifting from the power paradigm to the co-creation paradigm. As the company culture opens up, we are challenging ourselves to involve customers and experts at every stage. Deep insight is essential for us to design experiences that are desirable, seamless and memorable."*
>
> Laura Taylor, Director of Design Exploration, Philips Lighting[16]

15. Principle 7 (value-driven) deals in-depth with the concept of 'customer insight' and the 'customer insight trajectory'.
16. She said this in an interview with TheCoCreators

Target group connection as a basis for repositioning kids' magazine Okki[17]

Starting in 1953, for the cost of 15 cents per volume, publisher De Spaarnestad distributed two new magazines at Dutch elementary schools: Okki for the lower school classes, and Taptoe for the higher classes. From 1966 until 2009 these magazines were published by educational publisher Malmberg in the Dutch city of Den Bosch.[18]

Throughout these years Okki's formula remained largely the same. However, towards the end of 2007 it was evident that the magazine needed a facelift to stop the downward trend in subscription numbers. Over the years, new competitors had risen, not only in the direct field of kids' magazines, but also in the wider competitive environment of spare time activities in general, including television and gaming. Kids' frame of reference had been drastically reformed. By 2007 kids were used to fast-paced cartoons with edgy characters and intense story lines, and their lives were much more hectic and on-the-go than in 1953. Okki's artsy illustrations, text-oriented sections, and close-to-home topics lacked relevance and appeal for the new generation.

Malmberg started Okki's repositioning with an intensive customer-insight-trajectory. The editors immersed themselves into the world of six through eight-year-olds. They visited families inside their homes, accompanied them to sports clubs and other spare time activities, spent days in classrooms and at schoolyards, and analyzed all popular kids media. This immersion resulted in personas for the Okki target group, as well as the following key insight: "I'd like to be bigger." This served as input for a brainstorm session, which consisted of the editors, a target group expert, and a 'wild goose' – a creative thinker who didn't have to do anything with magazines, nor kids. The brainstorm yielded a wealth of ideas. The editors summarized and visualized these, and the involved target group expert discussed them with children.

The new concept was a success, but a learning of the team was that they could have gone a step further in engaging the target group. Although children as end-users were actively involved in the process, they did not participate in the brainstorm. In hindsight that would have been more efficient and more effective. Not only are children – unbound by life experience – the best 'wild geese' one can imagine, they would have also been able to sift irrelevant ideas from the funnel before they got elaborated on. For instance, during the brainstorm, grown-ups came up with a concept of a world in which everything was opposite to the normal world. Whereas adults had a lot of fun playing around with this idea, the level of abstraction proved to be way over the head of most 6 through 8 year-olds, and Blink had to let go of this concept.

17.   Stefanie Jansen, Kids & Family Insight, was involved in this case as target group expert. More information can be obtained from Jorien Castelein, director and co-founder Blink

18.   Lees hier meer over de geschiedenis van Okki: http://bit.ly/2f7bgfQ

Okki covers before and after the repositioning: volume #13 2008 and #11 2009

Customer connection as a basis for co-creation

For co-creation to occur, *real* understanding of the end-users is necessary. This involves knowing what motivates them, what their lives look like, why they do what they do. It is impossible for a group to come up with a relevant solution for a challenge without a shared understanding of end-users' related perceptions and behaviors, and of the drivers a potential solution might activate. Such deep understanding does not just follow from a survey or desk research; total immersion in the end-users' life is necessary – a so-called 'customer insight trajectory'.

> ❝ *I don't just talk a lot with youth; I observe them in their own environments as well. Sometimes I can see better what's going on than they can because I have more distance.*"
> *Fatima Fattouchi, Manager JIP Noord*

When organizations start a co-creation process without deep customer understanding, the first sessions will quickly spiral into a qualitative market research, focused on gaining the necessary understanding. This causes two problems.

First, a group interview is not the best means to get to deep understanding. An interview will activate end-users' frontal cortex, their *thinking mode*, from which they give verbal descriptions and explanations for their behavior. To really understand what they do and why, it is much better to observe end-users in their own surroundings.

Second, conducting exploratory market research when co-creation was expected can cause delusion among the participants. *"The output of the session is disappointing,"* is a frequently heard remark after a first brainstorm session with end-users, which turned out to be an exploratory focus group. Therefore, expectation management by the Co-creator is very important.

2.   What does active end-user involvement look like?

Conducting a creative process with a team may result in 'group think': falling in love and realizing group ideas without checking end-user relevance.[20] Adding end-users to the co-creation team will diminish this risk, but not eliminate it; as group members they are susceptible for group think, too. Thus, it is important to keep involving 'fresh' end-users. End-user involvement can take various forms, depending on the phase of the process and the intended role of the end-users.

CASE 22

The Heineken Nightclub of the Future emerged from co-creation with clubbers[21]

In 2011 Heineken and InSites Consulting decided to develop an innovating 'nightclub experience'. For this occasion, a dedicated design team was appointed, consisting of nineteen young talents from the four 'design capitals' Tokyo, Milan, Sao Paulo, and New York. These designers were crowdsourced through Facebook and local Pecha Kucha events.[22] The team was completed with several senior designers - both Heineken employees and freelancers. At the same time, 120 clubbers from the twelve trendiest cities in the world were invited to participate in a closed community, where they shared their clubbing experiences, reflected on the role of clubbing in their lives, and built on each other's ideas about the ideal nightclub experience. They answered questions, kept a photo diary, interacted with each other, and provided feedback on the design team's first sketches.

From the community's input, Heineken and Insites Consulting extrapolated 28 insights, which they translated to particular nightclub experience challenges. The design team and online community were to work together in coming up with solutions for these challenges. An example is the frustration caused by endless waiting to order a drink at a busy bar. A conceptual solution is a bar with a bottle-shaped icon. When guests touch the icon, it pulsates so as to grab the bar tender's attention. Heineken implemented the co-created solutions in a pop-up night club, which toured the world. The club attracted many visitors; more than 13.000 during Milan's Design Week alone! Visitors evaluated the experience with a 9 on a 10-point scale. This co-creation effort also yielded a lot of free publicity and had a positive influence on the beer sales: The Netherlands, UK, Czech Republic, and Poland saw an increase of 40%. InSites Consulting was rewarded the CCA Co-Creation Award 2011.

66 *Three success factors for innovation are empathy, diversity and incubation. Co-creation provides an exciting answer to all of these factors. Heineken executes this particularly well in their Open Design Explorations program. From emphasizing with their leading-edge consumers and taking their journey as a starting point, to bringing together a diverse group of young design talent. Not just during a one-day workshop, but in a year-long collaboration."*
Thomas Troch, Business Director, InSites Consulting US

Heineken Nightclub of the Future – online community

19.   Quote from a Designweek article: http://bit.ly/2wZ8u34

20.   More information about 'groupthink' can be found here: Janis, I. (1972), *Victims of Groupthink*. Houghton Mifflin Company, Boston. pp 223 of 't Hart, P. & Irving L. (1991) Victims of Groupthink, Political Psychology Vol. 12, No. 2, pp. 247-278 http://bit.ly/2y0FNzm

21.   More information about the Heineken case can be found here: http://bit.ly/2y7T4qN

22.   A Pecha Kucha is a visual presentation within seven minutes, consisting of twenty visuals that are each verbally explained in twenty seconds. More information can be found here: http://www.pechakucha.org/.

There are various ways to involve end-users in complete co-creation

Below we give an overview of various ways to realize end-user involvement. We don't intend to be complete, but to illustrate the diversity of available tools and techniques. A combination is always best.

Desk research and surveys

Desk research can provide a quick and broad understanding of a certain topic.[23] This type of research can be conducted safely and efficiently from behind a desk. Because the information can paint a lively image of end-users, desk research may be confused with actual end-user involvement. However, end-user involvement only occurs if end-users are directly questioned, at a minimum through a survey. We advise to always add face-to-face end-user contact. That will yield a much deeper target group gutfeel than a few diagrams!

Street research

Street research involves conducting brief, semi-structured interviews with end-users in their own surroundings. It typically takes place at a public space which attracts a large number of end-users, such as a shopping mall. However, any online or offline place with lots of end-users will do: think multi-player games, social media channels, health clubs, schools, public transportation, etc. Street research often yields fun movie clips with end-user quotes that are perfect for presentations. Because of the spontaneous character of street research, it is not suitable for deep conversations with end-users. To do that, more elaborate qualitative market research is necessary.

Traditional market research

Traditional market research is divided into qualitative and quantitative research. The difference is in the number of participants and the process. Quantitative research should always have enough participants to allow for statistical analysis. Moreover, the questioning process should be standardized so that results among participants can be compared. Qualitative research, on the other hand, uses smaller sample sizes since its objective is to gain a deeper understanding – the 'meaning behind the numbers'.

Quantitative market research

Quantitative market research can – among other things – deliver a quantification of market potential, guidelines for price levels, packaging cues, and shelf placement. Additionally, it can provide insight into the effectiveness of communication at a conscious, as well as a sub-conscious level.

Quantitative information may be necessary for creating support among stakeholders, for instance investors and business partners. Moreover, when an organization is interested in winning 'best introduction' in their field, quantitative information will be required.

The data yielded by quantitative monitors can also be helpful for marketing and PR, as well as to motivate employees. Finally, this type of 'hard' information is perfect as a baseline assessment on central parameters such as sales, awareness, image, and client satisfaction. When repeated at regular intervals, a quantitative monitor is born.

A golden rule when designing quantitative research or briefing an agency, is that the best research imitates reality as much as possible. This means that it is better to measure end-users' behavior, than to ask them for their judgement. In the end, what end-users think of something is of much less relevance than whether it works. Does it trigger their interest and do they take action?

Even if the end-product has not been developed, quantitative research can provide insight in the willingness to purchase, related to the optimal price level. This can be done, for instance, by measuring the response to conceptual packaging on real or virtual shelves, or the response to a brochure or website that explains the offer.

Qualitative market research
Historically, qualitative research is conducted in a laboratory setting, where a moderator interviews individuals or groups of respondents while they are being observed through a one-way mirror or closed TV-circuit. In addition, an increasing number of market research agencies offer tools for conducting online qualitative market research. However, for those with time to spare and an adventurous mindset, participating research is the preferred way of gaining insight. This is often referred to as 'consumer safaris': visits to end-users' own environments, both offline and online.[24]

Diaries, mood boards, and crowdsourcing
Especially when only quantitative market research is conducted, or qualitative market research in a laboratory setting, it is a good idea to have (part of) the respondents carry out a home-assignment to gain a better picture of their real lives. They may keep a photo and video log, make a mood board (possibly by using Pinterest), or share certain things through a smartphone app or social media platform.[25] There are various apps for sharing photos and

---

23. Principle 3 (ongoing) deals with desk research.

24. More information on customer safari's can be found here: De Bonte, A., Fletcher, E. (2014). *Scenario-Focused Engineering: A toolbox for innovation and customer-centricity.* Microsoft Press. Chapter 5: Observing Customers: Building Empathy. P. 123.

25. More information on different qualitative reserach techniques can be found here: Hanington, B., Martin, B. (2012). *Universal Methods of Design: 100 Ways to Research Complex Problems, Develop Innovative Ideas, and Design Effective Solutions.* Beverly MA: Rockport Publishers. And here: Sanders, E., Stappers, P. (2013). *Convivial Toolbox: Generative Research for the Front End of Design.* Amsterdam: BIS Publishers.

videos, some of them offering connected survey modules.[26] Should more mass be necessary, crowdsourcing techniques, such as contests, can be added.[27]

Quick checks

During a development process, the co-creation team will regularly want to get input on certain things from end-users and key players, without organizing a full-blown meeting. The team may need a response to different varieties of logos, names or pictograms, reactions to flyers or a website pop-up. For this purpose, a discussion group on an existing or private online or mobile platform is ideal.

> 66 *We frequently used our WhatsApp group and the Facebook group to quickly get some input from youth and others on things we were working on. That way, we would usually gather a lot of feedback from a large group of people within no time."*
> *Martine Jansen, former Co-creator JIP Noord*

Brainstorms with end-users

Brainstorm sessions are commonplace in organizations as a means to generate new ideas. Research, however, suggests that individuals can generate just as many ideas of at least the same quality.[28] The primary value of a brainstorm session then, is not efficiency or even effectiveness; it is its social function. Participants tend to feel content with both the process and the outcome.[29] Thus, brainstorm sessions are strong team builders. A successful brainstorm session delivers a feeling of group pride as well as a broad acceptance of the generated ideas.[30] At a later stage this will boost implementation.

Given the social function of a brainstorm session, it is important to give conscious consideration to the participants. Which group needs team building? Which stakeholders from inside and outside of the organization will be involved in the implementation of the outcome? Which crucial parties might resist implementation?

---

26. Examples of such apps are: www.contextmapp.com and www.experiencefellow.com

27. More information on crowdsourcing can be found in the introduction of this book.

28. More information on brainstorming can be found here: Sandberg, J. (2006, 13 Juni), *Brainstorming Works Best is People Scramble For Ideas on Their Own*. The Wallstreet Journal. http://on.wsj.com/2x31pw2 More can be found here: Williams, R. (2012) *Why Brainstorming Doesn't Improve Productivity or Creativity*. Psychology Today. http://bit.ly/2flc79i

29. Read more about participants' evaluation of brainstorming here: http://bit.ly/2f6WF3N and here: https://buswk.co/2x26vsr

30. Principle 6 (supported) deals with creating support for complete co-creation.

> ❝ *During brainstorm sessions the atmosphere is very important,*
> *especially when the participants are very different from each other.*
> *Everyone needs to feel safe to contribute. A good moderator will*
> *therefore work hard to establish a constructive atmosphere."*
> *Fatima Fattouchi, Manager JIP Noord*

Other than stakeholders and key players, it is a good idea to always add end-users to a brainstorm session. This guarantees that their perspective will be central to the idea generation, and will fuel target group gutfeel. For a typical brainstorm session with four to twelve participants, adding two to four end-users is plenty. They should be typical for the described target group and should be enthusiastic about participation. When two or more end-users participate in a group, they will respond to one another, which will deliver instant insight in the relevance of ideas for the intended target group. When a group exceeds twelve participants, it may be split in smaller groups with two to four end-users per subgroup.

CASE 23

D-reizen involved clients and other relevant parties in brainstorms about the future

In the summer of 2016 the Dutch travel agency D-reizen organized several brainstorm sessions with some of their own employees, business partners, a visualizer, and various end-users (travelers). The objective was to generate concept starters (rough concepts) for the future. In an interview with TheCoCreators Danja Lekkerkerk, marketing manager at D-reizen, explains why they invited customers to the sessions: "Nowadays the consumer determines the future, especially in retail. Fail to satisfy their needs, and you will lose them. That is why we involve customers in concept development, both for our stores and for our products. It is new for us to work this way, and that can make some people feel insecure. However, D-reizen is fifty years old and so much has changed in the travel industry during that time – the traveling itself as well as the way people book. It is only natural that we should change, too. Change may be scary, but if you want to survive, it's necessary."
Lekkerkerk feels that the sessions have yielded a wealth of ideas. "A few new ideas are directly applicable. Some of those are minor changes that make a huge difference for the customers. Other ideas we already came up with ourselves, but were confirmed by the customers and fine-tuned with them. And some of the ideas we had executed in the past; those have to be revived! Finally, customers came up with things we already do; apparently we have to communicate those better."
Lekkerkerk is enthusiastic about involving a visualizer: "Including someone who makes immediate sketches of the ideas is great. This makes ideas visual and easy to explain to internal and external people. Huge added value!"

Hackathons, challenges and battles

An interactive group approach, such as challenges, battles or hackathons[31] usually works stimulating for the participants and typically yields lots of new ideas, especially when there is time pressure.

Hackathons, challenges, and battles are complete co-creation when the teams incorporate people from the initiating organization, end-users, and other relevant parties. Often, however, the teams are homogeneous, usually consisting of a-typical end-users like whiz kids, trend setters or creative people. In such cases, end-users do play the role of developers, but not in co-creation. That is a pity because the initiating organization and other relevant parties can't add their knowledge and experience. Moreover, a lack of support for the solutions developed may occur when strategic partners and key players have been excluded from the process – the so-called 'not-invented-here-syndrome'. In that case, the ideas will not come to fruition, regardless of their quality. That is killing for the motivation of the creative team.

Minimal Viable Products (MVP's) and beta versions

More and more organizations experiment with launching a 'lean' solution or beta-versions at a premature stage. A lean introduction is the most basic variety of the intended solution, also referred to as a 'minimal viable product' or MVP. An MVP is directly accessible to all intended end-users, whereas a beta-version is only accessible for a pre-selected group of beta-testers, who provide the organization with their feedback for optimization.[32]

Both the introduction of an MVP and the use of beta-versions can be regarded as real-time experiments, delivering valuable information for the widespread introduction of an optimized variety. In both cases, relevance and appeal of the solution are inferred from real user behavior, with user response guiding optimization. When the group of consumers or beta-testers is large enough for statistical analysis, quantitative research is possible.

Advisory council

A growing number of organizations install an advisory council consisting of end-users. Such councils are consulted about the organizations' products, services, and marketing activities, give guidelines for improvement, and identify new challenges. Regularly consulting an advisory council through multiple online, mobile, and offline channels will keep it active. In addition, a council can be asked to perform dedicated assignments, such as keeping a photo and video log, describing trends, mapping competitors, and coming up with new ideas for marketing campaigns.

---

31.   The term hackathon was first used by developers of Open BSD during a development event in Calgary in 1999. More information can be found here: http://bit.ly/2wrD7KO

> ❝ *A customer advisory board helps organizations understand the motivating factors which are driving their customers' decisions and is therefore a crucial part of successful innovation.*"
> *Maria Letizia Mariani, President Philips Lighting Europe and Board Member Prysmian Group*

Because the council's views are not representative for the entire population of end-users, it is important to combine their input with data from other measuring instruments, such as quantitative monitors.[33] Moreover, we suggest adding other relevant parties to the council, so that multiple perspectives will be included in its advice. It is practical to invite people who have participated in a prior co-creation trajectory, as they know the organization from within and are likely to be motivated to add to its success.

End-users can play five different roles during complete co-creation

There are five different roles for end-users to play in a complete co-creation process: 1) informant, 2) inspirator, 3) co-developer, 4) co-producer, and 5) evaluator. Seldom do they play only one role at the same time. Usually, they are informants and inspirators in the beginning of a co-creation trajectory, and gradually evolve into co-developers, co-producers, and evaluators. Complete co-creation only happens when end-users also fulfill the roles of co-developers and co-producers.

The five roles of end-users

informant

evaluator

inspirator

end-user

co-producer

co-developer

---

32. More information about lean introductions and 'minimal viable products' can be found here: Ries, E. (2011). *The Lean Startup: How Constant Innovation Creates Radically Successful Businesses. Penguin Books Limited.*

33. Principle 3 (ongoing) deals with measuring instruments that can be used to track a solution's performance after implementation.

End-users as informants

As informants, end-users consciously add their perspective, knowledge, and experience to areas relevant to the challenge at hand. This information is necessary to decide whether to enter a co-creation trajectory or not. For instance, the challenge may have been defined in terms of an unmet need. If end-user contact shows this need has been met after all, co-creation is unnecessary. Does the need proof to be valid, end-users as informants will deepen the understanding of related drivers and barriers, and will help position conceptual solutions within their lives. Only concepts that resonate with central drivers and with the potential to play a structural role in end-users' lives are worthy of further investment.

CASE 24

Tesco did what Webvan dreamed of – for a fraction of the costs[34]

June 1999: the online supermarket Webvan opened its virtual doors to the American public. Webvan offered customers an online ordering system with delivery at the same day. In order to realize this promise, more than 800 million Dollars had been invested in automatized storage, delivery vans, a website, a multi-media marketing campaign, a loyalty program, and more than 400 employees. Webvan's CEO said in Forbes magazine: "Webvan will set the rules for the largest consumer sector in the economy."[35] Despite customers' enthusiastic response, within two years Webvan was bankrupt. The supermarket had forgotten to determine who would be its loyal customers, what would motivate them to buy at Webvan, and how to reach them. As a result, Webvan was unable to manifest the predicted revenues. Around the same time the British supermarket chain Tesco was conducting an elaborate research into its customers' needs and wishes with respect to online shopping. Tesco used its physical supermarkets as vantage point for the online version, and by 2002 it had created a profitable online business for just a fraction of Webvan's Dollar investment.

Involving end-users as informants is not only important at the start of a co-creation trajectory, but throughout its entire course. Their unique perspective is crucial for understanding the role that concepts and prototypes may play in their lives. Similarly, only end-users themselves can convey the different ways in which a marketing campaign may resonate with them.

> 6 9 *You can be surprised by the difference between how as managers you imagine people live, use services, and connect with their friends, and the reality.*
> *Mark Watts Jones, Director of Products at Myriad Group, ex-Orange[36]*

End-users as inspirators

The role of end-users as inspirators is intertwined with their role as informants. Typically, end-users will hop from one role to the other and back again. While end-users in their role of informants are approached as experts in their field, as inspirators they are encouraged to 'just be themselves'.

End-users can inspire subconsciously by just living their lives, oblivious to the fact that employees of the initiating organization and other relevant parties are observing them as they go about in their normal offline and online realms. They can also consciously agree to participate in ethnographic research. Then they will allow a visitor to enter their physical or virtual environment, and show their significant things, places, people, and activities. This active sharing of the end-users' world will be an ongoing source of inspiration for the visitors – long after the visit still – and the memories of these visits will act as a constant reminder to keep adding the end-users' perspective to the co-creation process.

Broad observation, without a structured agenda, is the designated method to get inspiration from end-users' lives. When observers take everything in like a sponge, open and unbiased, they will realize later on how they were inspired and where inspiration is doing its work. Usually, a visit to an end-user starts out open, for instance with a tour by the end-user, often concluded with a semi-structured interview about the challenge. Thus, in one visit the end-user first fulfills the role of inspirator, and then acts as an informant.

In addition, end-users as inspirators can be asked to complete creative assignments, like making a mood board about their lives or keeping a digital photo and video diary, possibly through a smartphone app, online survey tool, or a social media group. Finally, end-users will inadvertently keep inspiring while performing other roles, just by doing and saying things from their unique perspective.

CASE 25

Nike+ provides Nike with a unique peek in end-users' lives

Nike+ is an online platform developed by Nike, where end-users can create a free Nike+ account which allows them to follow their own sport endeavors. The data to do this is gathered by various devices and software, such as the activity tracker FuelBand and the Nike Running App. Through Nike+ Nike has established various active communities for clients that are looking to share their goals, struggles, and results in their particular sport (from running to playing golf) with friends and strangers. Thus, Nike+ provides Nike with a unique peek in end-users' sporting reality, as well as an enormous, always up-to-date database with workout statistics of all sorts of end-user types.[37]

End-users as co-developers

Co-creation only happens when end-users play an active role as co-developers. When end-users have the needed knowledge and skills, they may help develop a prototype or marketing campaign. But also when they are only indirectly involved with the production or shaping of a conceptual solution by adding ideas and feedback, they are engaging in co-creation.

CASE 26

Co-creation with seniors: developing the Helping Hand app [38]

Financed by a British county, the grocery shopping app Helping Hand was co-created by a group of roughly fifty 65-plussers, the IT-company RedNinja, and the Plus Dane Group, a local housing organization. In an interview with TheCoCreators, RedNinja's 'Co-creation Lead' Ashley Culvin explains: "Part of the seniors was skeptical in the beginning; they thought we wanted to sell them something. We started a dialogue with them, and explained that our goal was to make digital services more accessible for seniors. During these conversations, many seniors told us that they don't feel heard, and that even their own family members often don't listen to them. Thus, they really appreciated us asking them for their needs, wishes, ideas, and opinions. This resulted in more than 300 interested senior visitors at our kick-off event. One and a half years later, towards the end of the project, about fifty of them were still actively involved."

An evident need had to do with grocery shopping. Culvin: "Because of health and mobility problems, the target group often has difficulties with going outside and carrying heavy groceries home. Therefore, home delivery is ideal for them, especially when the weather is bad. Still, at the start of the co-creation process, only 5% of the more than 300 involved seniors indicated to have experience with online grocery shopping. Worries about online privacy and insecurity about their own online shopping skills were real barriers. During the process we saw their trust grow."

Over the course of several sessions the entire grocery shopping app – from functionalities to design to usability, was co-created with seniors. RedNinja's 'open innovation lead' Bridget Waters: "The seniors were in the lead, and helped us create a valuable, accessible, and relevant service."

The involved seniors are satisfied with both the process and the result, which clearly reflects their suggestions, ideas, and feedback. Irene, one of the seniors, enthusiastically evaluates: "That you can view the various parts of a grocery store simply by touching the screen.. I was really surprised about how fast and easy it is! And that is because they asked us, right? They kept asking us what we wanted, and how it should work for us!" Waters also identifies a marketing benefit resulting from the approach: "We are receiving an overwhelming response to this project. Whenever we visit events there is always someone who has heard of Helping Hand and wants to know more. It is the seniors that spread the story and generate interest!"

End-users as co-producers

End-users as co-producers stay involved with implementing the solution after its development and launch. They can play a role as volunteers, freelancers, interns, or employees. For instance, the JIP Noord location is always co-run by an intern earning study credits. Alternatively, a youth center in Amsterdam works with points that youth can earn by making themselves useful; with those points they can pay for their consumptions in the center. And *bliep, a mobile provider for youth, opened its offices for youth interested in gaining work experience in the fields of marketing, sales, innovation, managing, and customer services.[39] Part of these youth were helping *bliep for fun; others received financial compensation

---

CASE 27

Giffgaff works with clients as co-producers

"I am amazed that it actually works," said Mike Fairman, CEO of the British mobile telecom provider Giffgaff in an interview with the British news medium The Telegraph.[40] "When we started we were worried that we, as an operator, didn't have a call center. It all sounded a bit strange." Giffgaff, which set out as an experiment in 2009, by now has surpassed more than 160 competitors with a combination of low prices, no contracts, and a fair treatment. Nowadays, it is one of the biggest providers in the UK. Giffgaff is a mobile virtual network operator (MVNO), which means it is using an existing network, namely O2's. Giffgaff's business model is built on the premise of user community contribution. For instance, all online questions are answered by Giffgaff users, making a call center obsolete. Moreover, existing clients actively add new 'Gaffers' to enter the network, and come up with new strategies to help the organization grow. Roughly ten percent of all user ideas are implemented. Fairman: "The community decides by voting." In exchange for active participation Giffgaff clients can earn 'payback points', which they can cash out twice a year. Customer loyalty was illustrated by a recent incident during which the entire network was out because water had leaked on the servers. "Normally, that would have been a reason for acute provider switching, but our community stayed loyal to us!"

---

34.   More information on the Webvan case can be found here: Blank, S. (2007). *The four Steps to the Epiphany: Successful Strategies for Products that Win.* Hoofdstuk 1: The Path to Disaster.

35.   This quote is from a Forbes article: http://bit.ly/2wYWgHG

36.   Quote from: Ind, N. Fuller, C. Trevail, C. (2012). Brand Together: *How Co-Creation Generates Innovation and Re-energizes Brands*, Kogan Page, London. Page 2.

37.   More information about Nike+ can be found here www.nike.com.

38.   More information on the Helping Hand case can be found here: http://bit.ly/2x1Zmbe

39.   More information on the case *bliep can be found in principle 4 (productive), and: http://bit.ly/2wYWCht39.

40.   The interview with Mike Fairman (dd. 26-05-2015) can be found here: http://bit.ly/2wrRKgn

Co-ownership

One step further than having end-users co-produce a solution, is promoting them to co-owners. This has a positive effect on their motivation. After all, co-owners share responsibility for the results and will be driven to gain success.

Co-ownership can take various forms. Cooperations work with a passive form by giving end-users shares. An active form is giving them decision making power, for instance by making them members of the management team. Several forerunners, for instance the Spanish company Mondragón, are experimenting with these various forms of co-ownership.[41] Mondragón is a conglomerate of 257 organizations in the financial, industrial, retail, and knowledge sectors. All employees are co-owners and directly influence the company's decisions.

At this point, co-ownership of the organization is too much for most. Co-ownership of a co-created solution is easier to realize. That means that all involved parties can claim a co-created solution's success. They may be rewarded with a job in a co-created service, may form the interview committee for selecting new personnel, or can become members in an advisory council. It is good practice to clearly define the boundaries of co-ownership before starting a co-creation trajectory and to co-produce plans for co-ownership with all involved parties (including end-users).

We expect that co-ownership will become more widespread in the near future. For organizations seeking ways to guarantee taking end-user perspective serious in all organizational decision-making, co-ownership is the answer. However, these ultimately involved end-users will not stay representative for the entire population, so involving 'fresh' end-users on a regular basis remains important.

End-users as evaluators

Throughout any co-creation process, the co-creation team will want to check the relevance and appeal of the conceptual solution and its many aspects among end-users who have not been involved in prior stages. These end-users play the role of evaluators. They can do that at a conscious or subconscious level, with subconscious evaluations being the best predictors of actual behavior. A growing body of research shows that human behavior largely results from subconscious processes, rather than conscious analysis.[42]

The so-called qualitative 'test', whereby end-users are asked for their opinion of a stimulus, brings them in a conscious state of mind which does not parallel their normal, mostly unconscious decision making processes. Mapping their primary response will yield data with more validity. That can be done in a quantitative-experimental way, as well as qualitatively.

An example of the prior is the structural measurement and analysis of customer response after introduction of an MVP or beta-version. An example of the latter is the mind-mapping of spontaneous reactions to a stimulus as gathered for instance during a street research or through a mobile platform.

The combination of a quantitative experiment, completed with several first reactions as gathered by a street research or mobile platform, is the most efficient and effective way to get meaningful end-user evaluations. In a complete co-creation trajectory, extensive qualitative market research is not necessary, since the frequent end-user contact will yield plenty of qualitative information about the relevance of the solution and the place it may take in end-users' lives.

3.   How to find, activate, and reward end-users?

Where can one find end-users? What are they willing to do? How to motivate them? We often encounter these questions. Below we will try to answer them. Keep in mind that the practical details will be different in every unique co-creation endeavor.

Finding end-users

An unequivocal target group definition in terms of demographical, sociological, and psychological characteristics is a necessary starting point when aiming to co-create with end-users. Then, desk research can provide an overview of the primary end-user finding places: online and offline locations where they tend to gather and channels to communicate with them. Respondent selection agencies are specialized in this and can save a lot of time. However, as they are paid per participating respondent, the costs can mount quickly, also because the respondents from their panels are used to generous rewards in cash.

In order to cut costs, organizations can take end-user recruitment in their own hands, for instance by connecting to local clubs, adopting 'test schools', visiting discussion forums or launching crowdsourcing activities. Moreover, conducting a street research at the start of a co-creation process is a smart way to find end-users that may want to stay involved, while at the same time gathering basic end-user insight. It is important to realize that end-user recruitment takes a lot of time and is only successful when the organization is willing to structurally appoint someone with the time and resources to make it happen.

41.   More information about Mondragón can be found here: http://bit.ly/2x2tlQv and here: http://bit.ly/2y7StFy

42.   More information about the power of our subconscious can be found here: Mlodinow, L. (2012), Subliminal: *How Your Unconscious Mind Rules Your Behavior*. Vintage Books, Random House, Inc. New York, United States.

Activating end-users

Activating end-users is done by giving them interesting assignments and acknowledging the value of their input. It is important to keep in touch regularly, at least with a process update and preferably with a concrete question. This way, they will feel involved and are likely to respond swiftly to the next question or assignment. Predictability quickly becomes boring, so a mix of various forms of interaction is best: from a yes/no question through Facebook to a photo assignment via WhatsApp, to a work excursion with people from the initiating organization and other relevant parties, to a serious meeting.

Rewarding end-users

The most powerful incentive for anyone, including end-users, is the idea that one matters. Consistently approaching end-users as valuable partners – regardless of their age and background – will entice them to give their best contribution. Taking end-users seriously involves making them part of the challenge, sharing relevant information, regularly informing them about the process and the role of their input in it, showing appreciation, and always taking care of excellent catering during meetings. In addition, it works well to give them presents every once in a while. Depending on the end-user group, these can be flowers, a bottle of wine, a luxurious dinner or a gift card for a popular store or web shop.

In many cases, attention, appreciation, and regular presents will suffice, especially if the required time investment of end-users is relatively small. However, when they have to do quite a lot of work, are adding significant value, or having problems staying on task, a tangible reward is appropriate. It is important to prevent participants from feeling unappreciated and spreading negative stories about how they were used.

When the initiating organization takes care of end-user recruitment, it can be creative with the rewards. Coupons, tokens, points, vouchers, a free training or consult, a job, a free product – all of these are possible. When end-user recruitment is done by a selection agency, rewards have to be cash or can be transfered by bank by the agency. In that case, the Co-creator will negotiate an appropriate incentive with the agency.

CASE 28

Youth were intrinsically motivated to co-develop JIP Noord

Youth participating in live sessions at the city quarter's office usually received an incentive, for instance a €15,= gift card for a two-hour session. In addition, they spent a considerable amount of time co-developing JIP Noord via email, social media, and WhatsApp without expecting anything back. They said they were not involved with JIP Noord because of the incentives, but because they felt they were working on something big and important for all youth in Amsterdam-Noord.

> 66 *I think it's really cool that I am allowed to work on this. I feel I am doing something useful, something that will help others, too."*
>
> *Callum, 19 years old, co-developer JIP Noord*

4. Can other methods replace end-user involvement?

Despite the benefits of productive collaboration with end-users, other methods are often used instead. The most prevailing are: 1) creative sessions without end-users, 2) consulting target group experts or spokesmen, 3) consulting the sales department or customer service, 4) consulting one's own social environment, and 5) market research. Organizations have successfully used these methods *instead of* complete co-creation for decades. However, in the co-creation paradigm they should be used in *addition* to productive collaboration with end-users and other relevant parties.[43]

Creative sessions without end-users

Involving relevant stakeholders in creative sessions stimulates support for the creative process and its outcome, but has no influence on the relevance of developed solutions for end-users. That is why it is important to add target group expertise to the sessions – not (just) a target group expert who knows a lot about the intended end-users, but end-users themselves. What may help with the acceptance of adding end-users to a creative session is having them participate during just a part of it. When end-users participate at the beginning, this will leave time later on for the other participants to evaluate their input.

Consulting target group experts or spokesmen

Consulting target group experts – people who know a lot about a certain target group, such as child psychologists, teachers, or sports coaches – helps to form meaningful hypotheses. The same is true for consulting spokesmen for a certain target group, such as chairmen of student fraternities, religious leaders, and founders of fan groups.

Based on their knowledge and experience, target group experts and spokesmen are able to give a quick overview of target group characteristics. Their input during creative sessions is often valuable because of their unique perspective as bridges between 'their' target group and the rest of the world. Moreover, they tend to have a large, relevant social network, which may come in handy at a later stage.

However, It can be dangerous to blindly follow whatever target group experts and spokesmen say, because their vision does not always represent the reality of the average

---

43.   Our view on why co-creation is the answer to the current time-frame can be found in the introduction to this book.

target group member. Used to acting as authorities or activists, they tend to present their strong opinions about the target group as facts.

> ❝ *Sometimes you just have to try something new and see how it works. It isn't always what you expect. I usually have a good idea for what works with youth because I spend my days amongst them, but I still get surprised by how things work out with them in reality."*
> *Fatima Fattouchi, Manager JIP Noord*

Confessions of a target group expert

Stefanie Jansen, co-author of this book, used to work for kids market research agency KidWise. She confesses: "For years I was considered an expert on kids and family marketing, without having children myself. Only when I became a mother I realized the immense difference between knowing a lot about motherhood, versus being a mom. It is impossible for a not-mom to understand how subjective, irrational, and blurred by love the relationship between mother and child is.

Many childless young women predict that they will become consistent, fair moms. Very few succeed. Nowadays, most women turn out to become so-called 'spoiling' or 'influencing' mother types, despite their resolutions. This tendency has been going on for years, and has been described by me in presentations and reports, long before I became a mom. But the insight I used to connect to it – modern moms are afraid of confrontations – is wrong.

All mother types, including the spoiling and influencing moms, regularly face confrontations with their children. The reason that today's moms are more inconsistent than they would like to be, giving in more often than they thought they would, is that they sometimes need to let go. Not having to be the perfect mom, just being a woman for a moment is only possible with a content child. Giving in to the need to feel at peace happens daily in a split second, and is usually later compensated for by doing something very responsible for or with the child.

The ongoing balancing one's own needs as a woman with the drive to do what's best for the children is a very interesting source of inspiration for product and service development. So-called compromise products that combine playing with learning, safety with adventure, and health-boosting with indulgence are popular for a reason. Why? What driver do these products activate? The harmonious family, like I used to stress when I was still a childless target group expert? Or the independent woman, enjoying her own company and temporarily blissfully free from the heavy responsibility of motherhood, knowing that her kids are safe, healthy, and learning useful things?"

Target group experts

Target group experts know a lot about their target group and usually feel connected to it, but are not always part of it. Therefore, even if they *are* technically part of it, they still cannot be considered representative target group members. Their expertise makes them conscious of their own attitudes and behavior, which causes them to have other ideas and make other choices than the average target group member.

Target group spokesmen

Although target group spokesmen are part of the target group, they distinguish themselves from it by a relatively large societal involvement, passion, and assertiveness. As spokesmen they find themselves outside of their tribe. Their life looks very different from that of the typical target group member. They place themselves in different situations and engage with different groups. Thus, consulting a target group spokesman is not the same as involving average target group members.

> ❝❞ *Knowledge institutes often ask me to say something about parents. I usually do that, but I always wonder why they don't seek contact with parents themselves. I mean, I am a parent, too, but I am not the 'immigrant parent' they are interested in, or the 'lower SES parent' or the 'parent with young children'."*
> Jan Willem Roseboom, Founder and Director of Dutch parent network Family Factory[44]

Consulting the sales department or customer service

When developing solutions for challenges that have to do with end-users, it is good practice to keep regular contact with the sales team and customer service. Employees from these departments have daily contact with end-users and clients that know end-users well. Thus, they are well equipped to help forming hypotheses.

Personally accompanying a sales representative or employee at the customer service department is always better than just consulting them. These people are not trained to delve for deep target group insights, but to solve problems or sell products or services. Their target group observations tend to be mixed with their own interpretations.

Accompanying sales representatives or spending time at customer service is a good way of getting target group gutfeel and forming hypotheses, but has limitations as well. These channels do not offer much space to go in-depth with end-users, nor are they fit for involving them actively in a creative process. Moreover, client service mainly deals with

---

44. More information about Family Factory can be found here: www.familyfactory.nu

end-users who are already clients (or were), and who have a question or problem – not the typical target group. And some sales departments do not have direct contact with end-users, but are business-to-business representatives, dealing with in-between agents such as store managers. Thus, always involving end-users themselves remains vital.

> 66 *We continuously observe in classrooms how students respond to our methods. What is their body language, how are they working (or not), to what extent to they understand and enjoy the material, and do they actually learn something from it? We use observations and discussions with students and teachers to funnel our concepts until they are relevant and effective. Ideally, I would work in an RV at a school yard. I can't imagine developing creative educational content in any other way."*
> *Hetty Hurkmans, Publisher at Blink*

Consulting one's own social environment

It is not uncommon to base decisions on one's own (youth) experiences or results from 'tests' among colleagues or members of one's own social environment. These are dangerous habits because colleagues, friends, and family members are usually not representative of typical end-users, and personal experiences tend to be biased. In order to prevent basing decisions on wrong assumptions, it is best to use oneself and one's own social and organizational environment for defining hypotheses only.

CASE 29

The marketing manager's son advises: pink chips bag for boys and girls

In the fall of 2001 two project managers working for the Dutch kids market research agency KidWise were invited to the headquarters of a leading chips brand for a research briefing. The enthusiastic marketing manager explained that he wanted to introduce a pink chips bag for kids. He expected pink to jump from the shelves, and appeal to boys and girls. Since his own son loved pink, he had no doubt that boys would embrace chips in pink. Because his team was not so sure of this, he wanted to conduct a sound market research to prove his assumption. Based on a quick desk research and a pragmatic 'waiting room check' among children participating in another research, KidWise was able to objectively show that the color pink is disapproved of by the majority of boys, and that moms with boys tend to overlook pink packaging. This 'marent' – a parent who happens to be a marketer – had to conclude that his son had a special color preference, and that it is dangerous to blindly follow one's own children's advice.[45]

Market research

Organizations frequently use various forms of market research in cases where productive collaboration with end-users could have taken place, and may even refer to this research as co-creation. Two typical examples:

1. developing a concept or prototype without end-user involvement and then checking it on relevance and appeal during a so-called 'test';
2. asking end-users for their ideas about a certain challenge and then using their feedback as a base for developing a solution.

In these examples, organizations are consulting or activating their end-users, but do not engage in productive collaboration. End-users only play a role at the beginning or end of a development trajectory, and the initiating organization does not always use the gathered insights or ideas.

> **66** *A focus group is not co-creation because the company does not bring its own competencies but is asking the consumers to bring theirs."*
> Bernard Cova, Professor at Euromed Management Marseille[46]

Falling back on market research rather than co-creation can have various reasons, which are usually related to history, political drivers, ignorance, and insecurity.

Market research because of history

When market research has led to success for decades, it is hard to let go. However, in order to stay ahead of competition and find answers to tomorrow's challenges, new methods are necessary. The sheer fact that end-users' knowledge and power are growing at an exponential rate should be a reason for giving them a voice. In addition, now that more and more organizations are embarking on the co-creation trend, end-users will expect more and more to be asked for their input. Doing so will quickly become a dissatisfier for them.[47] Thus, it is wise to make traditional market research more interactive, increase its frequency, and add more relevant parties – in other words, to evolve it into complete co-creation.

---

45. The term 'marent' is short for 'a marketer who is also a parent and thus believes that he knows how to do kids marketing without having to contact other kids than his or her own'. More information can be found here: McNeal, J. (1999). *The Kids Market: Myths and Realities.* Paramount Market Publishing, Inc.

46. He said this in an interview with Yannig Roth (2011): http://bit.ly/2xAcYhd

A new drink was quietly taken off the market

An ex-marketer from an international food concern was willing to anonymously share his experiences with the failed introduction of a new drink with TheCocreators: "A few years ago we identified an opportunity for a product playing into a specific target group's lack of energy. Building on our long experience with fruit products we decided to develop a fruit juice fulfilling this need for more energy. After doing target group research we developed a concept that was relatively easy to produce. Shortly thereafter, we launched our product. Unfortunately, that was not as successful as we had hoped, and within several months we had to take it off the market.

Looking back, I think we were steering towards a certain outcome. Our first target group research was aimed at confirming the need we had identified, rather than gaining deep target group insight. Later we discussed our concept with a handful of consumers, and to be honest, they were hardly enthusiastic. At that point, we just pushed through because we believed in it, and also because we were under a lot of pressure from the top to launch a new product as fast as possible. Maybe more marketing power could have created more awareness, but in the end a product needs to sell itself because it really fulfills a need – and I don't think our product met that criterion."

Market research because of politics

When an organizational culture is dominated by political games, end-users are often used to push personal ideas. In those cases there is no real interest for the end-users' perspective. It is all about the suggestion that they played an important role in finding the a priori preferred solution, the gathering of market statistics that underscore a concocted decision or the generating of positive PR. In such instances, market researchers may get briefed on the preferred outcome. It is not difficult to manipulate results by suggestive questioning.

Market research because of ignorance

An organization may believe in actively involving end-users, but not knowing how to start, may hire a marketing or market research agency. Chances are that the agency sets up a traditional trajectory, in which end-users play the roles of informants and evaluators, but not the roles of co-developers and co-producers. Although a growing number of agencies claim to engage in co-creation, this is often market research pimped with a few moments of direct interaction between end-users and organization.

---

47. A dissatisfier is something end-users have come to expect organizations to do. It is not a reason to stay loyal, but something they would become disloyal over if it was not offered. The term was first introduced by Herzberg in his Two Factor Theory. More information can be found here: http://www.netmba.com/mgmt/ob/motivation/herzberg/.

Market research because of insecurity

Finally, market research is regularly used as an oracle to base decisions on. Requiring research for every decision not only has a paralyzing impact on creative processes, but also negatively impacts the motivation and confidence of the involved employees. Successful organizations use multiple channels to *continuously* keep contact with end-users, only conducting market research when additional insight is necessary or to follow their performance on central parameters.

5. Questions to our readers

1. To what extent do you feel your organization has target group gutfeel, and in what ways do you think this could be continuously broadened and deepened?

2. In what ways do end-users have a voice in your work?

3. Did your organization ever avoid involving end-users in a development process? If so, how did it happen and why?

Principle 2: With end-users.
In complete co-creation,
end-users always play
a central role.

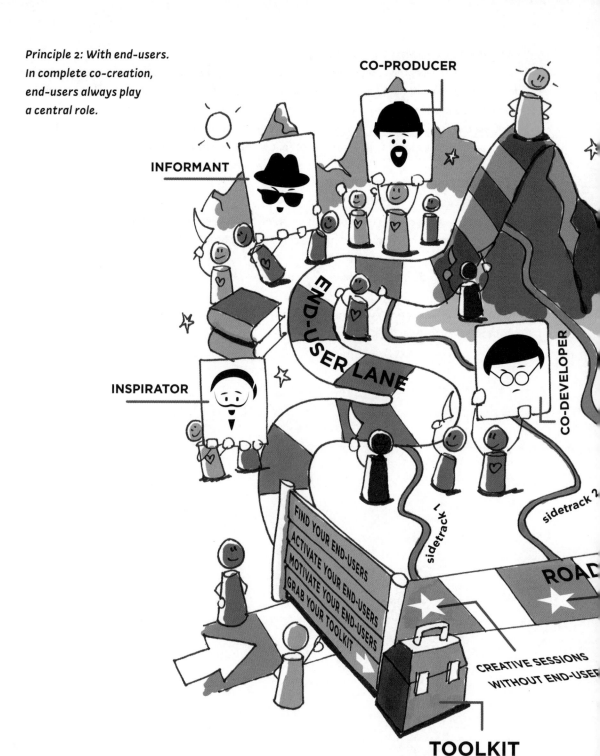

CO-PRODUCER

INFORMANT

END-USER LANE

CO-DEVELOPER

INSPIRATOR

sidetrack 1

sidetrack 2

ROAD

FIND YOUR END-USERS
ACTIVATE YOUR END-USERS
MOTIVATE YOUR END-USERS
GRAB YOUR TOOLKIT

CREATIVE SESSIONS
WITHOUT END-USER

TOOLKIT
TOOLS FOR END-USER INVOLVEMENT

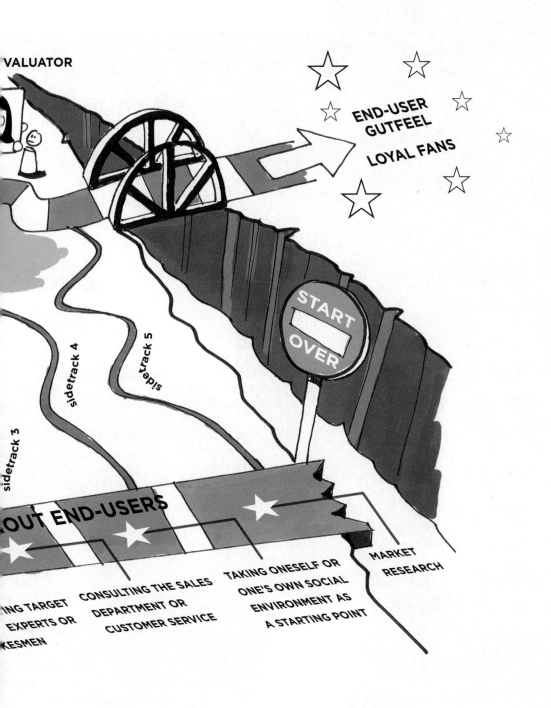

VALUATOR

END-USER
GUTFEEL

LOYAL FANS

START
OVER

sidetrack 5

sidetrack 4

sidetrack 3

...OUT END-USERS

MARKET
RESEARCH

...ING TARGET
...EXPERTS OR
...KESMEN

CONSULTING THE SALES
DEPARTMENT OR
CUSTOMER SERVICE

TAKING ONESELF OR
ONE'S OWN SOCIAL
ENVIRONMENT AS
A STARTING POINT

End-users and other
relevant parties participate
consistently in every
phase of the complete
co-creation process.

PRINCIPLE 3
ONGOING

Complete co-creation starts when someone, or a group of people, defines a challenge to be solved in co-creation. When carried out conscientiously, this process will result in the implementation of a co-created solution. Its continuous monitoring will lead to the definition of new challenges. Thus, complete co-creation is self-repeating and never ending.

This does not mean that every step will always take place with all involved parties. It should be a conscious decision to involve those that – according to the puzzle principle – will be able to add the most value at that time.[1] Only the participants in the co-creation team are involved in every phase of the development process; others may play a role in just one of the phases. In between the various group processes that comprise complete co-creation, the Co-creator will regularly spend time alone, for instance to write a summary of the findings, or to prepare a meeting with decision makers for the determination of next steps.

In this chapter, we do not intend to give a detailed description of the complete co-creation process. Rather, we want to make its continuous nature tangible. We will do this by first introducing the phase model "the Five F's", and then describing the co-creative elements for each of its phases.

Although the Five F model works well, a creative process does not have to follow these particular phases for it to be complete co-creation. After all, the primary difference between complete and incomplete co-creation is not the structure of the process, but the continuous collaboration of the initiating organization with end-users and other relevant parties. Thus, we advise organizations that already work with a different model to just keep using that. For instance, complete co-creation goes well with the agile processes (such as Scrum) that organizations are adopting rapidly.[2]

Reading guide for principle 3 – ongoing

By answering the following questions, this chapter describes the continuous process of complete co-creation in practice:

1. What does a process of complete co-creation roughly look like?
2. What are the co-creative elements of phase 1, founding?
3. What are the co-creative elements of phase 2, finding?
4. What are the co-creative elements of phase 3, forming?
5. What are the co-creative elements of phase 4, fine-tuning?
6. What are the co-creative elements of phase 5, following up?

As in every chapter, we will start out with the co-created youth information point JIP Noord as an example and end with three questions to our readers.

External parties participated in every phase of JIP Noord's development[3]

Developing JIP Noord was not a smooth process. The planning was subject to frequent changes, and in response to opportunities and barriers in the process, sub-steps got skipped or repeated. At several occasions, participants wanted to fall back to their routine, working with only direct colleagues. At such moments the Co-creator would remind everyone of the five phase plan they had committed to at the start of the trajectory. She would explain once more the role of end-users and other external parties in every phase, and the added value of that.

In the end, local youth and potential partners did actively participate in every phase: from designing the house style, physical space, website, and communication materials to thinking about the organizational structure, the services, products, and personnel, and from procedures for referral to external partners and privacy to activating social media and designing the opening ceremony.

The developed formula is a tailor-made JIP for Amsterdam-Noord, which can't simply be copied to other locations. A local approach is always necessary and the outcome can never be predicted.

1.   What does a process of complete co-creation roughly look like?

Complete co-creation follows the Five F's: founding, finding, forming, fine-tuning, and following up. This model is a loose guide to prevent ignoring crucial steps. Although skipping steps will almost always lead to a suboptimal result, conscientiously following the five phases is not a guarantee for success. In the end, success depends on the complementary knowledge and skills of the co-creating partners, the chemistry between them, and the competencies of the Co-creator.

The next page shows a schematic visualization of the Five F's, including the steps within each phase. The linear depiction of phases and steps may seem rigid. However, in reality various steps within phases will be carried out at the same time, and participants may start the next phase while wrapping up the prior one. Moreover, certain steps may take place implicitly, with others receiving explicit attention.

1.   Principle 1 (together) explains the puzzle principle.

2.   More information on agile processes and Scrum can be found here: Cohn, M. (2009). *Succeeding with Agile: Software Development Using Scrum*. Addison-Wesley Professional.

3.   Background information on this case can be found in the introduction to this book.

The Five F's, a phase model for complete co-creation

Founding	Finding	Forming	Fine-tuning	Following up
Step 1: formulate challenge	**Step 1:** broad understanding (divergence) - competitive analysis - market / trend analysis - target group analysis	**Step 1:** formulate co-creation challenge and define scope	**Step 1:** implementation plan	**Ongoing:** - (quantitative) tracking research - user council - community - continuous trend analysis
Step 2: formulate and support strategic objective and traction check	**Step 2:** deep understanding (convergence) - customer-insight-trajectory	**Step 2:** develop concept starters	**Step 2:** - concept optimization and production - (quantitative) product check	
Step 3: decide approach, yes / no complete co-creation	**Step 3:** insight generator - formulate key insight for each target group	**Step 3:** develop concept - (quantitative) concept-appreciation test / feasibility analysis / business plan - co-creation of marketing tools / launch event - if required, (quantitative) effectiveness check check marketing tools	**Step 3:** preparation introduction	
Step 4: decide directly and indirectly involved	**Step 4:** presentation research findings - first to small group of stakeholders - after formal go for all involved parties	**Step 4:** present concept - first to small group of stakeholders - after formal go for all involved parties	**Step 4:** launch event	

Implementing

go / no go   go / no go   go / no go   go / no go   go / no go

2. What are the co-creative elements of phase 1, founding?

The founding phase of a complete co-creation trajectory is successful when all directly and indirectly involved parties 1) share a sense of urgency around the challenge; and 2) are enthusiastic about complete co-creation as the route to the best solution.

A shared research experience

A first step in achieving this could be a quick research to show the challenge's relevance. This is usually a combination of desk and street research, possibly an online survey. Having stakeholders and key players conduct part of the research is a co-creative element with a positive effect on shared acceptance. This way, the research does not only yield the understanding needed, but also strongly enhances support for the co-creation process.[4]

An interactive kick-off session

A convincing kick-off session is a crucial booster for any co-creation effort, informing potential participants and motivating them to stay involved. Two co-creative elements determine the effect of the kick-off session: 1) diversity of the audience; and 2) interactivity.

Diverse audience

Anyone who may take the slightest interest in the challenge should receive an invitation for the kick-off session. The participants come from inside and outside of the initiating organization (including end-users!) and there is no maximum. Bringing together widely varying parties right from the start conveys an important message: everyone has a piece of the puzzle, so everyone is equally important.

Interactivity

Chances are that participants don't really feel at ease at the start of the kick-off session, especially when they are used to operating within homogeneous, familiar groups. Certain parties may not (want) to identify with the challenge. They may perceive it as an attack on their work or may be afraid that the solution will make their function or organization obsolete. Moreover, co-creation as the chosen approach may meet skepticism. Participants may be afraid to directly engage with end-users, may have had negative experiences with multidisciplinary teams, or may not believe that end-users can productively add to the development of a meaningful solution.

---

4. Principle 6 (supported) gives more information about involving stakeholders and key players as co-researchers as a way to boost support.

Philips Lighting actively involved end-users in the development of a new product[5]

"For the creation of a new product in the Philips Hue connected lighting range, the project team wanted to prevent getting stuck in our own tunnel vision, not putting the consumers first", says Niek Janssen, Global Product Marketing Manager, in an interview with TheCoCreators. "Even though we have lots of insights on similar products, you can't just use those exact insights for different use-cases and applications," André van Dijk, End-to-End project leader adds. "Experts and colleagues tend to push their own opinions, so direct customer connection is what we need if we want to continue offering the very best light experience."

Thus, Philips Lighting organized several brainstorm sessions with end-users and a multidisciplinary Philips team, representing product design, product lead, marketing, mechanical and optical engineers. "The engineers were specifically invited to participate, in order to make sure that they, too, would put themselves in the shoes of the customer while working on the product," says Miel Wellens, Industrial Product Designer.

The brainstorm sessions were conducted by an independent moderator with an experienced visualizer making sketches on the spot. The sessions yielded plenty of concept starters. "These first brainstorm sessions were very relevant," says Miel. "That is why we were motivated to keep involving consumers throughout the remainder of the project to make sure we were making the right choices. Because the whole team had been present during the brainstorms, everyone really wanted to work this way."

After evaluation on central parameters, Philips Lighting picked one of the concept starters as a starting point for the development of a prototype, which was then optimized in close collaboration with existing and potential HUE-customers in several countries.

The optimization sessions took place in end-users' homes to really understand how the product might add quality to people's lives. End-users were encouraged to play around with it so as to see the different light effects in their own environment, as well as identify potential practical barriers. Miel, André and Niek were present at these sessions, which were moderated by experienced local facilitators to guarantee a proper approach, structure and tools. "Even though the participating customers came from widely varying backgrounds and living situations, to our surprise their core motivations, needs, and expectations with respect to our prototype were very similar," Miel remarks. "This made it easy for us to make the right choices in finalizing the product."

The close collaboration with end-users had a strong impact on the final product. Niek explains: "End-users talk and think really different about products than someone who is involved in product development. This means that we had to leave some of our earlier assumptions behind, and that actually saved us money. For instance, one of our convictions was that we should produce two varieties of the product in order to appeal to the end-users' needs. However, they only needed one of these options, which allowed for a nice cut in production costs. We also learned that we have a tendency to make things rather complex for our end-users, simply because we have the technical capacity to do so. However, consumers really want things to be simple, and what is simple for us as experts, may still be complex to them." He adds: "We also learned about use-cases we didn't think of as important before, which for instance impacted the International Protection Rating of the product. This makes a huge difference! Also, the consumers' input helps us in developing our marketing strategy and tactics, such as how to use photography, video, description of the benefits, and other activation elements. We now know the words used by our target group. That makes it much easier to communicate. And finally, because of our direct experience with customers, we are well able to explain the choices made to our colleagues."

In effect, co-creating with end-users led to a doubling of the projected sales compared to the earlier stage business case. "Expectations are a lot higher now!" exclaims Niek enthusiastically. As a last tip, he adds: "It really helps to start involving end-users as early as possible, even before any product development has taken place. That simplifies the strategic decision making at the start of a product development process, has a strong positive effect on the quality of the first product propositions, and it makes the overall process more efficient, and also, more pleasant. It is a lot of fun working directly with end-users, and getting a peek into their lives!"

Examples of ideas visualized during the brainstorm for Philips Lighting

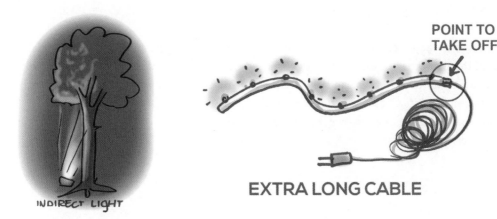

INDIRECT LIGHT

POINT TO TAKE OFF

EXTRA LONG CABLE

5.   The Philips team on this project consisted of: Niek Janssen, Global Product Marketing Manager; Miel Wellens, Industrial Product Designer; André van Dijk, End-to-End Project Leader at Philips Lighting; Vincent van Montfort, Mechanical engineer; Johan Ansems, Optical engineer. Stefanie Jansen, TheCoCreators was involved as a moderator, market researcher, and Co-creator.

> *An employee of one of the partner organizations kept his arms crossed for almost the entire kick-off session. He was against the development of a JIP, convinced that it would replace his organization. However, when he noticed that we were listening carefully to his ideas about the local youth and were taking notes as he spoke, he relaxed a bit. He accepted our invitation to take place in the advisory board and became JIP Noord's biggest fan. In reality, JIP Noord never threatened the existence of that organization; rather, the two organizations perfectly complement each other"*
> *Martine Jansen, former Co-creator JIP-Noord*

A diverse audience only has added value when the kick-off session allows for synergy between the various participants. Opportunity for informal exchange and networking is essential. In addition, recognizing and overcoming potential barriers is crucial. An interactive approach will help fuel enthusiasm. Having an important stakeholder introduce the challenge will underscore the importance of the co-creation trajectory. Inviting (local) media can help, too. Furthermore, having end-users present research results about the challenge and target group usually works convincing.

Making co-creation concrete helps fuel enthusiasm. Best practices can illustrate the role and time investment of different parties.[6] They will also highlight the differences between complete co-creation versus a 'standard trajectory', and show why co-creation is not only more fun, but also more effective.

A crucial interactive element of the kick-off session is gathering participants' existing ideas about the challenge, the involved parties, the end-users, and the market. Giving participants an opportunity to share ideas and really listen to them is essential to overcoming barriers. Because many different perspectives are present, a complete list of hypotheses can be made, in which everyone can recognize his or her input. That ensures that everyone will feel taken seriously.

6. The benefits of complete co-creation are explained in the introduction of this book. Principe 6 (supported) provides an example to illustrate them.

7. Principle 2 (with end-users) introduces the concept of 'key insight'. Principle 7 (value-driven) gives a step plan for verbalizing a powerful key insight.

3.   What are the co-creative elements of phase 2, finding?

The finding phase starts as soon as the co-creation team has been formed and ends when it has verbalized a powerful key insight.[7] This phase typically consists of five steps: 1) gaining a broad understanding (divergence); 2) gaining a deep understanding (convergence); 3) summarizing the findings of steps 1 and 2 in a report; 4) defining the key insight in a Key Insight Generator session(s); and 5) presentation of the results.

In this phase end-users play the roles of informants and inspirators. Ideally, there are a few in the co-creation team,[8] while most will be respondents in explorative market research.

Step 1: gaining a broad understanding (divergence)
The first step of the finding phase is dedicated to gaining a broad understanding of the target group, market, suppliers, competitors, trends, etc. The co-creation team does not yet focus on the challenge, but aims to paint a complete picture of the market situation. The co-creative aspect of this step is the fact that the co-creation team members are doing the research themselves, co-producing a summary of the results.[9] The Co-creator is the one keeping an overview, as well as the facilitator, motivator, and coordinator.

Customer connected organizations already have a broad and up-to-date understanding of the life and motivations of end-users and may be able to skip this first research.[10] This may also be the case when recent exploratory research has been conducted. However, avoid the pitfall of assuming to know it all based on old research! As a rule of thumb, go for an update when research has been conducted longer than a year ago.

Step 2: gaining a deep understanding (convergence)
The second step of the finding phase is all about gaining a deep understanding of the end-users as related to the challenge. Usually, a customer-insight-trajectory is needed. This involves immersion of the co-creation team in the end-users' world in order to understand their true motives. Depending on the intended target group, researchers may spend days in roadside restaurants, supermarkets or home supply stores, riding public transport or hanging out at a school yard, exploring an online multiplayer game or swiping through a dating site. In addition, expert interviews may be useful in this stage, or sessions with so-called 'unusual suspects'[11] – people who can shine a new light on a challenge from a different frame of reference. This type of research may cost quite a lot of time, but is essential to forming deep target group gutfeel.[12]

---

8.   Principle 1 deals with the co-creation team and why we recommend adding end-users to it.

9.   Teams that set out to gather visual data may benefit from mobile apps like: https://batterii.com.

10. Principle 2 (with end-users) deals with customer connected organizations.

❝ *It was new for me to do such an intensive insight-trajectory. I saw it as a great adventure, and was full of trust that this experience would help us develop a unique education method. And I was right! We came to a level of insight that we would have never achieved otherwise, and were also able to translate this to an innovative approach."*

Yvonne Gerridzen, former Publisher at Blink, about developing a high school method Dutch PLOT26 [13]

Again, the co-creative aspect is the fact that the co-creation team members conduct and report the research together. In addition, it is recommended to include other important stakeholders and key players in the customer-insight-trajectory. Direct contact between end-users and strategically important people stimulates support for the co-creation process and will help smooth implementation of the co-created solution. In order to eliminate potential barriers against direct contact with end-users, a workshop observing and interviewing can be helpful.

CASE 33

Blink periodically organizes a training 'observing and interviewing' for employees

Publisher Blink believes in customer connection and co-creation. Every employee has direct contact with students and teachers as end-users. Time is created for doing this, and there is also a team and a program to support Blink employees in working this way.

One of the elements in this program is a periodic training 'observing and interviewing' for all employees and partners directly engaged with the development of materials for children, parents, and schools. Separating observations and interpretations is a key topic, because direct interpretation obstructs the perception of business opportunities. The following example - an 'observation' with a limiting conclusion – illustrates this. The person writing down 'this family doesn't read' thought that this was an objective observation. However, it was an automatic interpretation, based on the observation that there were no books or magazines in the house. Taking this latter observation as a starting point would give rise to more inspiring implications with more opportunities.

11.   More information about 'unusual suspects' can be found here: Polhuijs, A. (2016). *Pionier!* Amsterdam: Boom Uitgers.

12.   Principle 2 (with end-users) explains the concept of target group gutfeel.

13.   PLOT26 was realized with the international agency Flare Innovation. This movie gives more information: http://bit.ly/2xnNh2o

Top line: limiting automatic interpretation and its implications; bottom line: pure observation and its implications

	observations *what someone said / did*	interpretaties *thoughts about why they did / said that*	implicaties *ideas about applications*
limiting	this family doesn't read	reading is no longer appealing to kids; parents no longer find it important	we need to stimulate reading and/or use other media than just print
promising	this family does not own any kids books or magazines. However, they do play casual games as well as complex multiplayer games which require a lot of reading (in English)	in order to understand the games, the children need to be able to read and write Dutch and English. They also have to be able to type	there might be a market for a 'gaming empowerment' proposition teaching children how to type, and practice their English and Dutch (including 'gaming jargon') to become better gamers

A customer insight trajectory is always tailor-made, its design depending on the target group and the challenge at hand. In order to realize the ideal mix for the given situation, the Co-creator (or hired expert) should have plenty of knowledge and experience with the specific methods and techniques. A lack thereof leads to a superficial or biased process, and increases the risk that the co-creation endeavor will yield a weak solution or no none at all.

Step 3: report

At the end of the research phase, the co-creation team bundles all data and understandings from steps 1 and 2 in a description of the market as related to the challenge and the (intended) end-users. To do this, they will first make an overview of all recurrent observations, and will then agree on interpretations and possible implications. Moreover, they will share the photos and videos yielded by the fieldwork. The Co-creator (or hired research expert) processes everything into a solid report.

The importance of a textually and visually strong and complete report should not be underestimated! It is a tangible evidence of the importance of the challenge and – when generously shared among all involved parties – it will feed target group gutfeel. The report (and accompanying photos and videos) is the basis that involved parties will fall back on during the entire co-creation trajectory – and probably long afterwards.

> ❝ *In the past we have done several innovations with an agency that never delivers reports. Now we can't find the insights that our concepts are built on. And we lost a lot of general target group information that could have come in handy now that we are re-considering our existing products."*
> *Innovation manager at a publisher*

More and more organizations work with target group personas and customer journeys. A persona is a description and visualization of the prototypical end-user.[14] A customer journey is a description and visualization of the process of choosing, buying, and using a specific product or service by the prototypical end-user. In a customer journey, 'touch points' reflect all contact moments between end-user and organization.[15] Personas and customer journeys can offer (future) business partners inspiration, for instance to determine a sales strategy, design an online platform, or develop a creative concept for a marketing strategy. Moreover, translating research results into personas and customer journeys is a fun team exercise and helps to make target group understanding tangible. Thus, it is a useful addition to the process of co-creative reporting by the co-creation team.

Organizations may skip the customer-insight-trajectory and simply hire an organization to deliver a persona and customer journey based on a 'black-box-procedure'.[16] When compared to the steps described above, this method lacks a team building aspect, hardly fuels target group gutfeel, leaves space for assumptions and discussion, and potentially fails to reflect reality, possibly giving rise to a potentially weak solution for the challenge at hand.

> ❝ *They paid some consultancy firm a lot of money to deliver a 60 page document based on desk research, containing target group personas and customer journeys. It looks thorough, but it isn't 'real' and it leaves way too much space for people's own interpretations. Reading that is absolutely NOT the same as visiting people in their own homes. I don't want any more 60 pagers, I want my team to get out there and see with their own eyes."*
> *José Manuel dos Santos, Head of Design Americas at Philips Lighting*

14. More information about working with personas can be found here: Revella, A. (2015). *Buyer Personas: How to Gain Insight into your Customer's Expectations, Align your Marketing Strategies, and Win More Business*. John Wiley & Sons, Inc.

15. More information about working with customer journeys can be found here: http://bit.ly/2f9RcJw and here: http://bit.ly/2eYATf2

16. Principle 5 (transparent) deals with the black box procedure.

Step 4: Key Insight Generator

A misconception is that end-users will provide a perfect key insight. This may happen, but usually the data about the target group contain only hints. The co-creation team will need to phrase the key insight during a Key Insight Generator. This starts out as a two to three-hour session, possibly followed by additional sessions. Participants are the co-creation team and potential others that were involved in the customer-insight trajectory.

At the start of the Key Insight Generator the participants will want to share their fieldwork experiences. After that they can start working as one team or in subgroups. First, they will filter a set of customer insights from the report.[17] This leads to a shared view of the deepest, central end-user driver as related to the challenge. This key insight is the basis for the co-creation of the solution and potential marketing tools.

Ideally, stakeholders and key players that did not engage in direct contact with end-users during the customer-insight-trajectory will still play a role in defining the key insight. They may participate during (a part of) the Key Insight Generator or are invited to give their view on the defined customer insights and key insight. This will help build their support for the co-creation trajectory and its outcomes.[18]

Step 5: presentation of the findings

In most cases, the Co-creator and several members of the co-creation team will present the findings to a small group of people, for instance a multidisciplinary advisory board or a group of stakeholders who are responsible for the go/no-go-decision at this point.[19] When a go has been given, it is a good idea to organize a second presentation for a large group of all directly and indirectly involved parties, including end-users. There should be plenty of opportunity for the attendees to mingle and share their thoughts about the findings and next steps. This is also a good occasion to invite them to participate in the next creative phase.

Having end-users present (part of) the findings and answering questions from the audience maximizes both the credibility of the research and the acceptance of conclusions and recommendations. Moreover, giving end-users a face and a voice will make it more likely for the other parties to understand the importance of their direct involvement, thus increasing the support for the co-creative approach.

17.   As mentioned in the introduction to this book, a customer insight is a deep understanding of the end-users and their knowledge, attitudes, and behavior as related to the challenge at hand. Principle 7 (value-driven) gives guidelines for verbalizing a strong key insight.

18.   Principe 6 (supported) deals with creating and keeping support.

19.   Principle 1 (together) and principle 6 (supported) deal with the multidisciplinary advisory group, which consists of stakeholders and key players and has a positive effect on their acceptation and support of the co-creation trajectory.

4. What are the co-creative elements of phase 3, forming?

The output of the forming phase is a translation of the key insight to a conceptual solution for the challenge at hand. This is done in four steps: 1) defining a co-creation assignment; 2) developing 'concept starters'; 3) funneling to a concept, and 4) presenting the concept. End-users play the roles of co-developers and evaluators, not only by (ideally) participating in the co-creation team, but also by helping shape the concept in various rounds.[20]

Step 1: defining the co-creation assignment

In preparation of the phase of concept development, the co-creation team will add market and end-user understandings – including the key insight – to the originally defined challenge. Then, the Co-creator will define a co-creation assignment, which describes the desired output (a solution for the challenge) in general terms. In order to stimulate out-of-the-box-thinking, it is important to refrain from filling in the road to the solution.
To verbalize an open assignment, it is helpful to phrase it as a 'how-question'. Any question starting with 'how' is an open invitation to freely explore the different possibilities. Potential preconditions may be added as clauses. When a clear co-creation assignment has been verbalized, the Co-creator will present it to the decision makers for approval. Should they give their 'go', the creative process can begin.

The first step is to determine which internal and external parties to add in this stage. Who exactly they are depends on the challenge and the needed expertise during concept development. Among them will always be various end-users. The selected participants will receive an invitation for a kick-off session, providing them with more information about the challenge, the co-creation assignment, and practical agreements about the creative process.

CASE 34

Example of a co-creation assignment
An organic, portion packaged cookie is sold in natural food stores. For the target group 'parents with children' the snack is hard to find in the stores, in part because it is hidden in the fridge. A group of parents and children was given the following co-creation assignment: "How can we ensure that these cookies grasp parents' and children's attention in the store, given the fact that they need to stay chilled?"

---

20. Principle 2 (with end-users) deals with the various ways of involving end-users.

21. More information on Battle of Concepts can be found here: http://www.battleofconcepts.nl/

Online crowdsourcing platform Battle of concepts[21]

Organizations looking for new ideas or creative solutions can use the online crowdsourcing platform Battle of Concepts to get help from college and university (ex-)students. As 'innovators' in the Battle of Concepts community, they can submit ideas or solutions to challenges posted on the platform by organizations. The platform sends these ideas and solutions to the organizations, which chooses the winner. Rewards vary from € 1.000,= to € 5.000,=.

Step 2: developing concept starters

This step often starts with one or more creative sessions with the co-creation team and added participants. Ideally, a visualizer is present to grasp ideas in images on the spot. Other, online possibilities are for the Co-creator to organize a challenge or battle, or to use crowdsourcing to generate a large quantity of ideas. Later in the creative process, these can serve as stimuli.

In a few rounds, potentially building on the catch from a challenge, battle or crowdsource, the co-creation team with added parties will develop the first rough solutions for the challenge at hand: so-called 'concept starters'. This usually happens during live brainstorms, but it can also be done online.[22] How many co-creation rounds are necessary to get to one or more concept starters, which creative tools to use and who to involve is impossible to predict. These are decisions that the Co-creator needs to make, based on the prior step's yield.

We recommend organizations to follow their own traditions in developing concept starters. If there is no tradition, remember to always make a visual and a textual summary of the concept starter. A visual summary may be a sketch made by a visualizer during a creative session, or a mood-board made by the co-creation team. For the textual summary, the following framework is useful:

·	Key insight: a deep driver for a target group, powerful enough to inspire new behavior.[23]
·	Benefits of the conceptual solution for the end-users.
·	Reasons to believe: the reasons why end-users would believe that the conceptual solution will indeed offer these benefits.
·	Selling idea: the main promise of the conceptual solution or the most important, unique benefit summarized in a catchy slogan.

22.	Principle 2 (with end-users) deals with live creative group sessions and the optimal amount of participants in them.
23.	Principle 7 gives guidelines for phrasing a powerful insight

Step 3: funneling to a concept

After developing one or more concept starters, the co-creation team will compare them along predetermined parameters, such as how much time and money are required for realization. Based on this analysis, they will select one or three concept starters and shape them into clear-cut concepts: verbalized and visualized potential solutions for the challenge at hand. Team members will confront 'fresh' end-users with these concepts, not to test their appreciation, but to gain a deep understanding of the relevance of these concepts in the end-users' lives. After all, only solutions with real relevance will stay successful in the longer run.

End-user response will determine which of the concepts to develop into a tangible prototype, dummy or demo. The co-creation team may make the prototype, dummy or demo, potentially in collaboration with external experts, or may supervise an external party doing it. The team will invite end-users that were not involved in the process to use the prototype, dummy or demo and to give tips for optimization. When numbers or an objective signature is needed to convince stakeholders, a market research agency may carry out a systematic quantitative concept appreciation test.

Step 4: presenting the concept

The formal wrap-up of the founding phase is usually a presentation of the conceptual solution to the decision makers, potentially solidified by a feasibility analysis or business case. Should they give their go to further development, a presentation for a large group of all the directly and indirectly involved parties should be organized. Again, in both settings it helps to have end-users conduct the presentation or parts of it.

5.   What are the co-creative elements of phase 4, fine-tuning?

The Co-creator starts this phase with making an implementation plan. This will guide several parallel multidisciplinary work groups to form and prepare the concept for introduction, including the co-creation of a launching campaign.[24] The Co-creator co-ordinates this process and makes sure that all deadlines are met. At the same time,

> ❝ It is very important to have someone keeping everyone else focused. Continually seeking contact, face-to-face but also online and mobile, does not only create a bond, but is also an alarm clock for the participants: 'Oh yeah, I was supposed to be there then and to finish this by then...' Especially when you are working with adolescents it is necessary to app them all the time. Even when they are motivated, they still tend to forget was agreed on."
> *Fatima Fattouchi, Manager JIP Noord*

he keeps working on support from stakeholders and key players.

The most involved end-users will take a seat in the work groups, thus playing the role of co-developers. Other end-users, not involved in prior stages, will function as evaluators of the solution and aspects of it, as well as evaluate ideas for its launching campaign. Even if the founding phase has yielded a very relevant and unique concept, letting go of end-user involvement in the fine-tuning phase can lead to a mistranslation of the concept to the final solution and launch campaign.

Step 1: making an implementation plan

Following the structure "who does what when", the implementation plan clearly describes the steps to take the prototype to market launch.[25] The Co-creator makes sure that the plan is always up-to-date and accessible for all involved parties. By structurally mentioning end-users as part of the 'who' in every step, the plan helps to secure end-user involvement in this phase.

Steps 2 and 3: preparing market launch

In this phase, several parallel opportunity work groups will optimize the various aspects of the solution (step 2) and prepare for launch (step 3). Depending on the solution, they may be grouped according to themes such as design, packaging, styling, shop floor promotion, stand design, website, social media, advertising, and launch event.

The co-creation team members divide themselves over the work groups, which are then extended with relevant internal and external parties and end-users. Each work group consists of all relevant parties: at least end-users, but also experts relevant for that work group. For instance, a work group concerned with the development of packaging may include a package designer, whereas a web designer and communication expert may be added to a work group focused on creating a new website. A precondition for the selection of these experts is that they are open to equal collaboration with end-users.

Although every work group is focused on a different aspect of the solution and its implementation, they all follow the same iterative co-creation process. In order to guarantee relevance and uniqueness, they use various channels to keep involving end-users as evaluators, possibly in the form of a quantitative market research, or connected to the launch of an MVP or beta-version.[26]

24. Principle 1 (together) introduces the concept of multidisciplinary work groups.

25. Principle 6 (supported) deals with the importance of a sound implementation plan in creating and sustaining stakeholder support.

26. Principle 2 (with end-users) deals with MVP's and beta-testing.

Multidisciplinary opportunity work groups with youth in action: briefing the architect and co-creating a logo for JIP Noord

Step 4: launch event

A launch event is an important part of the total marketing campaign around the introduction of the co-created solution and can yield strong free publicity. At the same time, it is a perfect moment for all involved parties to celebrate their success and motivate them to stay involved after launch. Thus, the development of the launch event – of course in complete co-creation with all relevant parties – deserves a lot of attention.

A launch event can take many shapes. It may be a symposium, a show, or an interactive experience. When it is not a public event, all directly and indirectly involved internal and external parties should receive an invitation, including a large group of end-users.

JIP Noord was officially opened by local youth

On a cold, wet day in January 2013, a colorful event took place to celebrate the official opening of JIP Noord. This event was prepared and carried out by local youth. They were the hosts, the ones thanking the various involved stakeholders and key players, the ones showing visitors around, the ones taking care of entertainment with music and dance, and the ones taking care of the catering with home-made exotic and Dutch food and drink. Visitors to the event didn't just see the result of a lengthy co-creation process – a brand new JIP Noord – but also gained insight in the unique way it was developed and a warm feeling about the local youth and their enthusiasm and creativity in developing and showcasting JIP Noord.

6. What are the co-creative elements of phase 5, following up?

The end-user focus may vanish after implementation of the co-created solution. Busy with practical tasks and not used to ongoing end-user involvement, organizations may forget to keep pulling them into an active role. To continuously feed target group gutfeel and optimally shift with the market tendencies, it is important to keep end-users actively involved in this phase.

To fuel customer connection, organizations may use various instruments, including tracking research, social media analysis, online communities and fan clubs, an ambassadors club, and an advisory council.[27] These are not co-creative per se, but they all help prove the long-term success of solutions that are developed in co-creation, and thus are necessary for co-creation to be successfully instilled in an organization.

Co-creative organizations periodically conduct meta-analyses on all monitoring instruments, and share their understandings with relevant internal and external parties. Such update-meetings tend to give rise to the identification of new challenges and new co-creation trajectories.

26. Principle 2 (with end-users) deals with MVP's and beta-testing.

27. Principle 2 (with end-users) deals with customer connection, tracking research, and advisory councils.

Ongoing citizen involvement to improve the quality of life in Reykjavík[28]

Better Reykjavík is an online consultation forum where all citizens, including politicians and civil servants, are invited to share their ideas on issues regarding services and operations for the City of Reykjavík, Iceland. "The initiative is a grassroots bottom-up design and not for profit all the way," says Róbert Bjarnason, CEO and co-founder of The Citizens Foundation, in an interview with TheCoCreators. "We started few weeks after the financial crisis hit Iceland in 2008, and launched Better Reykjavík early 2010, a week before that year's city elections. The financial crisis destroyed a lot of trust in companies, institutions and government. With Better Reykjavík we want to give citizens more influence, encourage better decisions and help build trust between citizens and government."

There are several processes running on Better Reykjavík: "The first is a classic agenda setting process where people can submit, debate and prioritize ideas about any policy in the city. The top ideas in twelve categories go on for processing by different city councils, for example the planning council or tourism council. At each stage of the process everybody that supported or opposed the idea gets an email about its status. People can participate through online apps on mobile devices or computers. Citizens also participate in face-to-face meetings and on other social media. This way we are always connected and people can share their thoughts anywhere, anytime."

The co-creation between citizens and government goes beyond submitting ideas: "We also have been running a participatory budgeting process where about 5% of the capital spending budget of the city is given directly to citizens. Since the start of this project in 2012, this has been about three to four million EUR per year. Citizens have three to four weeks to submit and debate ideas about projects that they envision in their neighborhood. Examples are skateboard parks, park benches, playgrounds, and pools. Then the city takes four to six months to evaluate the ideas and selects 25 ideas for each neighborhood to go into the voting stage, with each idea showing the cost in the user interface. The budget voting stage is the final co-creation step where each citizen selects a neighborhood and selects their preferred budget for their neighborhood by adding and removing ideas to the budget. This both gives us high quality citizen prioritization and teaches citizens about how much things cost to build and the fact that there is no unlimited budget and you always have to make compromises. It is very transparent!"

One of Robert's favorite stories is where a grandmother took part in the participatory budgeting process. "She was living in the west of the city by the sea where massive piles of rock protect the road from erosion. She said she would love to take her grandkids to the beach but she didn't trust herself to climb down the rocks. So she submitted an idea about building a ladder down to the beach. Other people supported it and enough people added it to their budget so it was voted in and built. Now a lot of people use this simple metal staircase, there is a Kindergarten close by and many tourists stop by."

People have responded overwhelmingly positive with participation growing each year. Over 70,000 people in Reykjavík have visited Better Reykjavík. There are about 100,000 people on the voting registry in Iceland. There are about 20,000 registered users, which is 20% of the voting population. More than 1,000 ideas have been accepted as projects to build and those have had a real visual impact on all neighborhoods in the city. A total of 6,772 ideas have been submitted with 15,225 debate points for and against the ideas.

At this point Better Reykjavík is mainly an extended concept forming platform. Citizens are not yet directly involved in the implementation of the ideas: "That is an area we want to improve in the near future. There is definitely strong demand for co-creation and participation from citizens and we are just starting!For now the ideas are planned to be as close as possible to the concept that came out of the debate process."

Right before closing the interview, Bjarnason excitedly wants to share his city's latest co-creation initiative: "The city of Reykjavík is now creating a new education policy for the year 2030, for city schools that cover the ages of 2-18. At this point, the citizens of Reykjavík have identified the key competencies that 18 year-olds need to have achieved when leaving the city school system at 18. Those have been debated and prioritized. Next step is this October where citizens will be asked to come up with concrete ways to achieve the most important competences. We are on our way to make this initiative a complete co-creation process!"

7. Questions to our readers

1. How does the development process described in this chapter relate to the processes you are used to work with?

2. Did you ever participate in a development process where steps got skipped? If so, which steps got skipped, why, and what were the consequences?

3. To what extent do you feel your organization is effectively staying in touch with developments in the market and among the end-users? What points for improvement do you see (if any)?

28. More information can be found here: https://betrireykjavik.is/

Principle 3: Ongoing.
End-users and other relevant parties participate consistently
in every phase of the complete co-creation process.

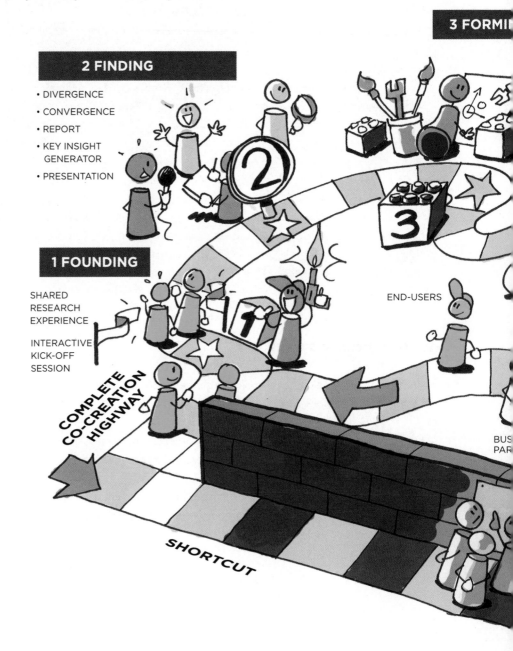

CO-CREATION ASSIGNMENT
CONCEPT STARTERS
CONCEPT
PRESENTATION

4 FINE-TUNING

- IMPLEMENTATION PLAN
- OPTIMIZATION
- PREPARE LAUNCH
- LAUNCH EVENT

LAUNCH EVENT

EXTERNAL
EXPERTS

BILD
EESE

DECISION
MAKERS

INTERNAL
EXPERTS

5 FOLLOWING UP

- TRACKING RESEARCH
- CONTINUOUS SOCIAL
  MEDIA ANALYSIS
- ONLINE COMMUNITIES
- FAN CLUBS
- AMBASSADORS CLUB
- ADVISORY COUNCIL

Complete co-creation leads

to implementation of the

co-created solution.

PRINCIPE 4
PRODUCTIVE

In theory, a process of complete co-creation does not stop after the stages of idea generation and concept forming, but continues until the co-created solution has been implemented (and even after that point). In reality, however, organizations often start a co-creation trajectory with vigor, only to abandon it half-way through. They may keep doing research and then pull the plug. Or the process may actually yield promising concepts – possibly even a working prototype – but because of financial, political, or other reasons, a real solution never comes to completion. In such cases, there may have been a co-creation process, but not a *productive* co-creation process, as it did not yield an implemented solution.

Organizations regularly claim to get stuck in a creative process because the results are not 'actionable'. We define 'actionable results' as: clear-cut interpretations of data that inspire and motivate to take further action.[1] Naturally, it helps when the presentation of the results has a motivating effect, but taking action ultimately boils down to taking responsibility. Results can be hugely 'actionable', when an organization does not take responsibility for moving from insights to solutions, the co-creation process will sooner or later come to a standstill.

A stagnant co-creation process is, obviously, a waste of invested time, means, and energy. So how can it be prevented? Stagnation of a complete co-creation process usually happens in the phases of finding and founding. Organizations either lose themselves in ongoing research, or they keep working on concept development, failing to take the plunge and implement the solution. Thus, it is important for organizations to stay alert to the following six signals of stagnation, and to take direct action if any of these occur:

· A competent Co-creator is lacking for the fine-tuning and implementation phase.
· The Co-creator does not have enough time, resources, or decision making power in the fine-tuning and implementation phase.
· The Co-creator is lacking support during the fine-tuning and implementation phase.
· Stakeholders and key players are not enthusiastic about the conceptual solution.
· More research is being conducted, even though a thorough understanding of end-users and market has already been established.
· Other projects are prioritized.

Reading guide principle 4 – productive
This chapter seeks answers to the following questions:

1. What are the main characteristics of a competent Co-creator?
2. How to empower the Co-creator?
3. How to support the Co-creator during fine-tuning and implementation?
4. How to deal with a lack of enthusiasm among stakeholders and key players?
5. How to prevent getting stuck in research or development?
6. How to prevent priority shifting?

As usual we will start this chapter with the case JIP Noord as an example and will conclude with three questions to our readers.

---

1.   More information about actionable results can be found here: Krizan, A., Merrier, P., Logan, P., & Williams, K. (2008). Business Communication. Thompson South-Western, Mason USA. pp. 83, KISS Metrics.

CASE 38

From hypothesizing about the needs of local youth to the opening of JIP Noord[2]

From the kick-off session up to the opening of JIP Noord it was clear to all involved parties that this was a collaborative project calling for an active attitude of everyone. It started with the Co-creator asking all attendees to the kick-off session to interview local youth about their need for information and consultation, and to share this information by means of a short report.

After people disliking this approach quickly abandoned the process, a loyal group of involved experts – some working for the city, others for other relevant organizations – and a group of local youth remained. Motivated by the idea that a group is more than the sum of its parts, and that end-users should always be the starting point for developing a new service, they kept showing up to add their knowledge, experience, and perspective to the process.

The enthusiasm of this co-creation team helped the Co-creator to stay positive, despite recurrent barriers on the road to implementation. She felt also hugely supported by the responsible policy advisor, who took care of all politic prerequisites for realizing JIP Noord. Some of the things that were taken care of on the top level included support from the alderman, sufficient financial means, and an assistant who was to carry out practical tasks during the phase of fine-tuning and implementation. Thanks to this assistant (who later became JIP Noord's manager) the Co-creator was able to stay focused on supporting the optimization process and preparing for launch.

1. What are the main characteristics of a competent Co-creator?

A competent Co-creator is able to keep a helicopter view over the entire co-creation trajectory and works steadily towards implementing the co-created solution, whilst motivating the participants. Bridging the gaps between the initiating organization, end-users, and other relevant parties, she plays both an operational and a managerial role. Without filling in this function, there is a real risk of leaving the co-creation principles along the process, or even abandoning the co-creation endeavor entirely.

Usually, it is not enough to simply appoint someone as a Co-creator. It is important to first establish whether the candidate 1) understands and supports the challenge at hand and the objectives underlying the co-creation process, 2) unconditionally believes in complete co-creation, and 3) knows what steps to take in a complete co-creation trajectory. In addition, she must be willing to relate respectfully to widely varying people, and needs to be able to guide a multidisciplinary team to their best performance. Only then will she be a motivating process catalyst, fueling productive collaboration until a solution has been implemented.

2. Background information about this case can be found in the introduction to this book.

The main distinction between a Co-creator and other project managers is their view of development processes. The Co-creator is more than others convinced of the importance of actively involving end-users and other relevant parties, and ideally has first-hand experience working this way.

Co-creator as a regular organizational function

Given the increasing importance of collaboration and co-creation, we expect that Co-creator will be a normal organizational function in the near future. To illustrate, publisher Blink now has a team of internal Co-creators that are responsible for facilitating the continuous co-creation between publisher and partner schools.

Some authors of case studies refer to all participants in a co-creation process as 'co-creators'. We prefer reserving this title for the process manager, because the success or failure of the co-creation endeavor is directly linked to this person. Other participants may have important input, but usually participate next to other activities, and although they may feel honored to part-take in the co-creation process, they don't necessarily feel responsible for its outcome. The Co-creator is the one keeping them involved and motivated, probing them for their input on a regular basis, summarizing it and translating it to the next step's vantage point.

The Co-creator's role is different in every phase of the co-creation trajectory. The stage of concept development calls for a combination of analytic and creative capacity, whereas the stage of optimization and implementation needs a Co-creator with skills in the realms of management, networking, planning, and co-ordination. There are exceptional people who have it all. Most of us, however, are either analytically or practically oriented.

Since complete co-creation ultimately needs to lead to implementation, it is important to screen candidates on their *practical* skills. When having to choose between an analytical, creative or practical type, go for the latter and realize plenty of analytical-conceptual and creative support. A result-driven, 'get-it-done' type is likely to be a more effective Co-creator than an enthusiastic concept developer, who may lose interest in the implementation phase or may get in trouble due to practical mismanagement.

The table below shows the 'need to have' and 'nice to have' characteristics of a Co-creator. The 'need to haves' are the minimal requirements to fulfill this function. The 'nice to haves' are necessary in complete co-creation, but can be added by colleagues or external experts such as a market researcher, innovation specialist, communication expert or (web)-designer.

Co-creator competencies

NEED TO HAVE	NICE TO HAVE
* practical orientation	* analytical capacity
* strong social antenna	* strategic insight
* political sensitivity	* research skills (capable of independently
* stress resistance and flexibility	designing, conducting, and reporting
* networking skills	qualitative and quantitative market research)
* (project) management skills	* knowledge of and experience with designing,
* able to lead and motivate multidisciplinary	conducting, and analyzing customer insight
groups	trajectories
* basic research knowledge (to purchase and	* knowledge of and experience with creating
interpret market research)	online and offline user platforms
* basic knowledge of concept development (to	* experience with end-user recruitment
brief external experts)	* knowledge of and experience with creative
* basic marketing and communication	techniques and concept development
knowledge (to brief external experts)	* knowledge of and experience with the
* knowledge of the possibilities for conducting	development and implementation of marketing
online and offline creative processes	tools
* modest personality: takes pride in	* experience with recruitment of new personnel
facilitating others to shine; does not have to	
be the focus point of attention	

When the initial Co-creator does not implement the solution

Ideally, the Co-creator is responsible for the process from the first exploratory research up and including the implementation and monitoring of the solution. However, in reality the first three phases are often conducted by an internal or external concept developer, who delivers a concept and then leaves the process. At that point, responsibility for optimization, implementation, and monitoring of the solution is either shared by a self-managing team[3] or assigned to someone else – possibly a busy manager who was not involved in the prior development process. Both options carry a risk of stagnation due to a lack of focus and ownership.

3. More information about self-guiding teams can be found here: Vermeer A., Wenting, B. (2014). Zelfsturende teams in de praktijk. Reed Business BV. And here: http://www.scrumguides.org/scrum-guide.html.

The main characteristics of a competent Co-creator

(project) manager

knows about creative processes

social antenna

does not give up easily

enthusiastic

stress resistant

networker

modest

knows about research

practical

flexible

knows about marketing and communication

politically sensitive

motivator

knows about concept development

Involving the implementer on time

Should the person responsible for concept development not be the same as the one responsible for implementation and monitoring of the solution, make sure to involve the implementer at an early stage. After the implementer has observed the process for a while as a passive participant, he will gradually evolve into a coordinating manager. Then, after the transition of the founding phase to the fine-tuning phase, the first Co-creator (the concept developer) steps back. Ideally, he or she will still be passively involved as the 'conscious' of the co-creation trajectory, making sure that the challenge, key insight, and conceptual solution will be the guiding principles during optimization and implementation.

By involving the implementer early on, he will feel part of the co-creation process, internalize target group understanding, and learn the ins and outs of the conceptual solution. That practically reduces the risk of stagnation to zero. However, from a cost perspective, organizations may add him only after the concept has been delivered, or maybe even (partly) implemented. In that case, the selection process of the implementer is the key to success.

Selecting a good implementer

General rules for the recruitment of new personnel apply to the selection of an implementer. Think of making a clear-cut function profile and testing candidates for key competencies. In addition, we recommend involving the first Co-creator (the concept developer), end-users, and other relevant parties that played an active role in the prior development process in the selection procedure. They know best what kind of person will be most successful in implementing 'their' solution. Moreover, involving end-users in the procedure will yield direct insight in the way in which candidates relate to the target group.

CASE 39

Involving consumers into the recruitment of personnel

As part of the ongoing collaboration with consumers, The Royal Melbourne Hospital now involves them in recruiting their workforce. In an interview with TheCoCreators Rhiannon Beggs, Allied Health Manager – Speech Pathology & Audiology, explains: "I personally always held a firm belief that for healthcare to be truly patient-centred and responsive to the community in which it serves, it has to place patients and carers at the fore-front of everything. This includes integrating patients in re-designing services, reviewing processes, and selecting the workforce. As a trained Speech Pathologist I am frequently reminded of how essential successful communication is to guaranteeing positive health outcomes. Screening candidates on patient engagement is very valuable!"

To ensure support within the organization, a clear strategy was put in place. Then, the project team developed procedures to make working together easy as possible for staff and consumers. "Staff workshops were conducted and training was provided on identifying potential consumer representatives and working with them in staff recruitment. But also, how to provide and receive feedback," explains Beggs. Training was also provided to the new consumer representatives: "This involved understanding of our department of 275 FTE in the wider organization and educating them on the Melbourne Health Partnerships in Care strategy, The Allied Health recruitment model focusing on values and interview tips. Depending on confidence level and previous recruitment experience all consumer representatives were provided with one-one support by myself on their first 1-3 interview panels."

To date consumer representatives have sat on over 70 recruitment panels. Beggs: "Being the lead on this project has been an extremely rewarding experience. Consumer representatives provide a different perspective to staff that have been embedded in the business of providing patient clinical care for some time, and bring plain common sense. Staff members have reported that they have unexpectedly appreciated the types of questions consumers ask. Perhaps most importantly, consumer involvement in staff recruitment helps to demonstrate to candidates that the Hospital takes consumers seriously."

When asked about lessons learned Beggs adds: "I've learnt it is important to treat consumer representatives as you would other staff. Due to the size of our organization it can be a pretty daunting place, so I make every effort to introducing our representatives to as many people as possible in order for them to feel part of the team. It is not uncommon to see a consumer rep roaming the halls chatting to staff now which is just wonderful to see. I've also learnt that the process needs to be supported heavily from the top. Without the Director of Allied Health supporting our vision we would have had an extremely difficult time convincing all staff that this initiative would enhance their recruitment experience."

A survey was conducted in February 2017, revealing that 90% of senior staff members felt there was clear value of involving consumers as co-recruiters. One respondent commented: "To me, seeing the candidate interact with the consumer was the most valuable aspect of having them on the panel.

2. How to empower the Co-creator?

Just appointing a Co-creator – even a competent one – is not enough to secure concept realization. Empowering him with the time, resources, and decision making power needed to implement the concept is essential. If he is expected to run the implement process on top of his normal work load, the risk of failure is huge, because he will tend to prioritize his normal work. If he is denied access to the resources needed for implementation – usually money, but resources can also be materials or software – implementation logically will not follow. And when he is not granted sufficient decision making power, for instance when thick bureaucratic rules keep slowing him down, sooner or later he will lose his motivation.

4.   This case is based on a series of research concerning the functioning of the CJG's, that Stefanie Jansen carried out for De JeugdZaak between 2009 and 2011. For more information, see: www.dejeugdzaak.nl.

5.   Several cases and quotes in this book deal with aspects of the rise and fall or transformation of the Dutch Centers for Youth and Family (CJG's), in which various organizations in the field of youth care were supposed to collaborate.

CJG-coordinator, a hell of a job?[4]

In 2007, the Dutch minister of Youth and Family decided that all Dutch counties should found Centers for Youth and Family (CJG's) as physical locations in neighborhoods where parents and children could get information and advice with respect to growing up. The idea was that in these centers, all local parties in the fields of pedagogy, psychology, and youth health care would work together. In order to coordinate this collaboration, CJG-coordinators were appointed.

In June 2011 the newspaper Nederlands Dagblad wrote that CJG's often didn't get enough visitors. Since then, most CJG's have been reformed to neighborhood-based mobile teams, serving their target group in schools and other common finding places.

There are plenty of CJG's that attract a steady stream of visitors, though. These tend to be managed like independent stores with a CJG-coordinator who has been granted enough time, means, and decision making power to make his 'shop' successful. In other words: creating support at the top level to empower the CJG-coordinator is a prerequisite to a successful CJG.

However, in many cases the CJG was yet an extra task for people who were already very busy with other work, and had to deal with all kinds of bureaucratic procedures from the different partners in the CJG. This caused the burn-out or resignation of quite some CJG-coordinators before they were able to realize a successful center.

When the vision is clear and the county supports you in it, then CJG coordinator can be a super job, but when that foundation is faulty, you will have a very very hard time.[5] And if, on top of that, you don't really know much about the contents, you will quickly feel lost. There will be pacts among the participants that sabotage the collaboration process. Ultimately, partners will mentally disengage from it. They will pull back into their own organization, rather than focus on creating a successful CJG. That's what's going on here. We have a process manager who doesn't know anything about child and family care, and who is also lacking in communication skills. Her dominant attitude evokes resistance. When counties want to keep control, they need to appoint someone who is a strong communicator, yet at the same time able to take on a modest and facilitating stance. When you have faith in the joint power of the collaborating parties and you just want to serve them in making their best contribution, things should go rather smoothly."

Manager GGD (Public Health Service) of a Dutch county during the development of the CJG's (Centers of Youth and Family) in 2010

Supporting a Co-creator with time, resources, and decision making power follows from a conscious decision to invest in the co-creation endeavor. This may also entail the (temporary) change of organizational rules and procedures. Given these implications, the decision to invest in co-creation will only me made after sufficient support has been created for the challenge and the objectives, co-creation as the designated process to get to the solution, and the Co-creator as the responsible process manager.[6]

Time

It is important for the Co-creator to negotiate enough time for implementation of the co-created solution. Often, self-imposed time pressure results from hard agreements made about the launch, market introduction, or delivery. Such time pressure may lead to taking shortcuts in the development process, so-called incomplete co-creation.

Shortcuts may seem to save time at first, but often lead to a mistranslation of end-users' needs to a solution. They also tend to blur the traceability of a solution. While the relevance of an evolving solution for the intended end-users is always clear to everyone involved in a complete co-creation trajectory, shortcuts tend to obscure this understanding. After a shortcut has been taken, the conceptual solution may suddenly fail to fit end-users' needs, without a clear reason why. This will force the co-creation team to go back into the process to the point where the shortcut was taken, and start all over again. Such loops are a waste of time, money, and energy. Furthermore, they tend to have a negative effect on the team's motivation.

Aside from wasting time, energy, resources, and motivation, the consequence of taking a shortcut may be for the higher management to halt the co-creation process. Even if the original concept was relevant and attractive for the intended target group, the unnecessary expenses associated with the deviation from its premises may lead the organization to not give the co-creation team the opportunity to translate it to a winning market introduction.

In short: when a Co-creator experiences time pressure in a co-creation trajectory, he needs to fight the urge to either resign from the process or take shortcuts. It is better to negotiate with stakeholders about a more spacious planning.

Resources and decision making power

Ideally, the Co-creator will receive the necessary resources and freedom to make his own decisions, for instance to form his own implementation team. When the challenge is relatively small, such as the co-creation of a marketing campaign, this is should suffice. When it concerns the development of something bigger, like an entirely new product or service, it is often best to found an independent business unit or even a separate organization.

Startups tend to do this automatically, but when the co-creation process takes place within a large, established concern, the Co-creator is often treated like a normal employee. He may not have a budget for implementation and may have to follow all kinds of delaying rules and procedures. For those looking to maximize the chances of successful implementation, we recommend treating the co-creation process as a new business. This can be done right from the start, but the beginning of the fine-tuning phase is also a logical moment for separation from the mother organization.

JIP Noord as a semi-independent youth information point conducted by the city quarter

How to organize JIP Noord? That was a difficult topic. Various partner organizations indicated they would like to run it. However, this would pose the risk that the partner in charge would become too dominant. Moreover, it might cause jealousy among other partners. Neither scenario would be helpful in the necessary close collaboration.

JIP Noord as an independent foundation then? This was the scenario local youth were most enthusiastic about. They perceived this as the most objective scenario with the most freedom for JIP Noord to flexibly wrap itself around the needs and wishes of the end-users and stay on top of market trends. An additional benefit would be that foundations – as opposed to a city quarter – are allowed to acquire funding as extra financial means. A disadvantage is that founding a new not-for-profit poses various legal challenges and depends on government subsidies. Moreover, the city quarter has its own ideas about the information and advice function for local youth and young adults as a government task. An independent JIP could drift too far away from this vision.

A creative construction, conjured up by an independent expert in city policies consulted about this puzzle, is to detach a city worker as JIP-manager at one of the key partners. This key partner would run JIP Noord and, being a not-for-profit, would be able to acquire external funding, while the JIP-manager would report directly to Amsterdam-Noord.

The final choice of the city quarter was to directly employ the JIP-manager. He was allocated his own budget, location, and assistant, and was, to a large extent, free to shape his work the way he thought best for further development of JIP Noord. This way, Amsterdam-Noord would stay in control, with JIP Noord operating as a semi-independent information shop with its own style and procedures.

All involved end-users and key players accepted this outcome because they had been intensely involved in the decision making process, and understood that given the objectives, this was the best scenario for JIP Noord.

6. Principle 6 (supported) deals with the crucial role of support in a process of complete co-creation.

3. How to support the Co-creator during fine-tuning and implementation?

Whatever the solution, the way to implementation is always unpredictable and filled with obstacles. The process takes a large dose of enthusiasm and determination, and chances of success are limited when the Co-creator needs to pull the trajectory all alone. Appointing a Co-creator without an assistant and without allowing her to form a co-creation team comes with a real risk of burn-out or resignation.

Support by an assistant

In order to keep the Co-creator motivated and energized, he needs to feel free to focus on process facilitation and realizing prerequisites for implementation. This includes varying activities, such as the negotiation of deals with suppliers, distributers, or business partners, the realization of production locations, the preparation of an introduction campaign, conducting optimization research, and setting up a baseline measurement directly after launch. A Co-creator with a good assistant taking care of practical details is able to concentrate on such key tasks, and thus will be more effective. Typical 'assistant tasks' involve planning meetings, booking locations, inviting of attendees, arranging catering, recruiting end-users, setting up social media activities, and maintaining these.

Help from the co-creation team, advisory council, and work groups

A carefully composed co-creation team is not only necessary to represent the important points of view in the process, but also helps in creating support and filling in the Co-creator's need for colleagues and sparring partners. The co-creation team stays involved throughout the entire trajectory. In addition, an advisory council may add their ideas at regular intervals, and opportunity work groups will start preparing the solution for implementation in the fine-tuning phase. These teams can save the Co-creator a lot of work.[7]

CASE 42

At *bliep opportunity teams formed organically around needs as they occurred

Co-founder Jochem Wieringa explained in an interview with TheCoCreators how at *bliep opportunity teams formed organically: "Youth with an affinity for a particular topic would gather around it spontaneously. For instance, one of our guys thought it was time for a helpdesk through Twitter and founded it on his own accord. His friends started helping him, and thus they organized a smoothly operating Twitter helpdesk. We saw this happening, and facilitated them with the means they needed to optimally run their helpdesk. It really was theirs – a helpdesk for and by youth."

Given the importance of active involvement of colleagues and representatives of other relevant parties in the co-creation team and work groups, a prerequisite of successful implementation is that the managers of these individuals allow them enough time to participate. The Co-creator should realize concrete agreements about this with the managers of the relevant organizations, or have his own manager do this.

4. How to deal with a lack of enthusiasm among stakeholders and key players?

When decision-makers have been carefully taken along the process, chances are that they will embrace the co-created solution and give their blessings for implementation.[8] It does happen, though, that formerly enthusiastic stakeholders lose their interest. The Co-creator needs to be able to recognize that and respond swiftly.

Recognizing a lack of enthusiasm

When important stakeholders or key players respond negatively or neutrally to the conceptual solution as developed during the forming phase, alarm bells should go off. Even if they don't openly oppose, their lack of enthusiasm will seep through to the co-creation team and other involved parties. Chances are that they will resign from the process and that the solution will never see the light.

CASE 43

New CEO of a retail chain shows lack of enthusiasm for co-creation[9]
In an (anonymous) interview with TheCoCreators, the former Marketing Director of a large retail chain was willing to share her experiences with a prematurely halted innovation trajectory: "A specific client group realized 80% of our revenues, but in the five years after their initial purchase they never bought anything else. We identified this as a business opportunity and took on the challenge to develop something that would motivate them to come back and evolve into loyal customers. Our CEO saw the business opportunity, too, and agreed with our proposal, which entailed a large budget and a lot of hours of many people. We had assembled a motivated team with people from various departments, we had hired external innovation specialists to guide the

---

7. Principles 1 (together) and 3 (ongoing) deal with the function and consistence of the co-creation team, advisory council, and work groups and the importance of involving end-users in these groups.

8. Principles 1 (together) and 3 (ongoing) deal with identifying and involving stakeholders, such as the higher management, investors, co-producers etc. Principle 6 (supported) deals with creating and maintaining their support for the co-creation process.

9. Maarten Pieters, at the time part of the involved agency Flare Innovation, was part of the innovation team.

process, and we had designed a clear-cut action plan. We started with vigor, and after a few weeks of observing and talking to various clients, co-workers, and external specialists we had created several promising routes for innovation. The atmosphere was good and the preliminary results were refreshing and interesting enough to keep us going. Then everything changed. Our supportive CEO announced his leave, and his successor had very different ideas about the organization. This meant the end of our beautiful innovation trajectory.. I felt frustrated in the midst of this political power play that harmed our business, and left the firm shortly after this experience. Looking back it was a typical case of 'not invented here'. I don't think there is anything I could have done to revive the innovation process. What I did learn is this: when the CEO doesn't believe in it, don't bother!"

How to recognize a lack of enthusiasm? In part, this has to do with social intelligence and the ability to read non-verbal communication. Signs clearly indicating that enthusiasm is lacking are a closed body posture and negative facial expression. These may include folded arms, downward pointed lips, and a frown. More subtle signs are a neutral body posture and blank facial expression, or the absence of non-verbal signs of enthusiasm. When there are no sparks in the eyes, no upward pointing lips, and no wide arm movements, the Co-creator should be on the alert, especially when the questions asked are mainly critical rather than constructive.

Critical questions

Critical questions pertain to potential obstacles that may occur in realizing a concept. Usually, they are introduced with a short analysis carrying a negative conclusion in it. This is followed by the (rhetorical) question. The person asking the question takes a distance from the conceptual solution by phrasing it in terms of 'you', rather than 'we'. Some examples:

- "This reminds me of [... example of a failed project ...]. Back then we couldn't get the materials needed. How do you think to accomplish that now?"
- "You don't have any convincing proof that this will work, so who do you think will be crazy enough to finance it?"
- "Our organization has zero experience in this field. Don't you think it's safer to look for a solution closer to home?"
- "Most of our clients are not yet engaged in [... concept-related behavior, for instance social media or mobile ...]. Do you really think it would be a good idea to bet on that to change any time soon?"

Some critical questions will always be asked and are indicative of a healthy sense of realism. However, a lot of critical questions with an absence of constructive ones are indicative of the 'hang-yourself-method'. This is a Socratic conversation technique aimed to have the Co-creator convince himself that the conceptual solution is not realistic. It is an effective way to kill a concept before implementation.

Constructive questions
Constructive questions are indicators of enthusiasm. They pertain to the implementation of the conceptual solution and are often phrased in terms of 'we'. Several examples:

- "What do we need to realize this?"
- "How fast can we bring this to market?"
- "Where can we get the funds to make this happen?"
- "Do we already have someone to manage this?"
- "Would you trust us to run this project?"

Stimulating enthusiasm
When constructive questions are not being asked, it is clear that enthusiasm is lacking. In that case, it is imperative to voice this, to find out what causes it, and what is needed to regain trust. It may be useful to create a setting in which stakeholders and key players can engage directly with end-users to draw their own conclusions on the relevance and appeal of the conceptual solution for the target group.

CASE 44

Teacher reactions to concept lesson convinced stakeholders
During the customer insight trajectory that preceded the development of Groove.me, a method English for the Dutch primary education, the very first session with children was all about music. However, not everyone in the innovation team was instantly convinced that music would be a good vehicle for the development of a new education method. The most important question was whether teachers would accept such a method as educationally sound. That is why the innovation team developed a concept lesson and confronted teachers with it in the presence of crucial stakeholders and key players. Without exception, the teachers responded very positive. They instantly recognized the motivating power of music and could really see themselves happily using such a method. Based on these sessions a go for further development was obtained.[10]

10. This case was introduced in the introduction to this book. More information can be found here: www.groove.me and here: www.thecocreators.com/case-study-groove-me/.

Another proven way to secure enthusiasm among stakeholders and key players is to realize quick wins and share these with them. For instance, launching a beta-version or MVP in an early stage is a smart way to gain basic statistics and useful end-user reactions that can help convince stakeholders and key players of the relevance and appeal of the concept.

Using social media to connect end-users to the solution in an early stage is helpful, too. An overview of social media results, such as the number of members in a group, and end-user remarks after using the solution, can have a very convincing effect.

5. How to prevent getting stuck in research or development?

It is an understatement to call the step from concept development to implementation exciting. Where the finding and founding stages of a complete co-creation process safely take place behind closed doors, the fine-tuning phase will show the truth. Once a solution gets implemented, external critics such as end-users, journalists, competitors, and experts will judge it. Sales or visitor numbers and user satisfaction scores may quantify its success. This may lead to a scolding by the higher management, a bankruptcy or a success story.

Fear of judgment
The judgment that is inherent to the fine-tuning phase, may give rise to failure anxiety and an urge to keep swirling around in prior phases. It is tempting to keep re-shaping the concept, conducting yet another creative session, maybe having another designer make a proposal, or doing another research.

> 💬 *In my work you have to stay curious, keep doing research. Prior to every new decision or plan I ask several youth to think with me. When I do that I always make clear that I can't possibly always include all of their suggestions and ideas, and there are other parties to take into account, too. And everyone knows that in the end, I just have to decide something, otherwise nothing would ever happen."*
> *Fatima Fattouchi, Manager JIP Noord*

Repeated market research can seriously slow down a co-creation process. Moreover, rather than providing answers, such research may give rise to ever more questions. Seeking of end-user response when a sound concept has been delivered is a clear sign of stagnation.

---

11.   Principle 6 (supported) deals with creating and maintaining support among stakeholders and key players.

A private investor took his loss

A private investor assembled an innovation team to start a co-creation process with youth. Several rounds of sessions with potential end-users gave rise to a concept for an online youth platform. When it was ready to be introduced as an MVP, the team kept conducting sessions with youth to optimize it. Finally, to see if 'it would do something', the team launched a temporary website which explained the concept to the target group. At the same time, conversations with potential project managers and investors took place. The temporary website had zero effect, as the target group didn't know it existed. The conversations with potential project managers and investors were dead-ends as well; the people interviewed lacked the enthusiasm needed to commit. This was also true for the innovation team. Although they believed in the relevance of the concept for the target group, they viewed themselves as concept developers and not implementers. Finally, the private investor took his loss and closed the case.

Making clear agreements

To prevent getting stuck in research and development, it is a good idea to agree on the date and time for a presentation of the research findings and a presentation of the conceptual solution. Specify the parameters for evaluation of both research and conceptual solution, and set a date for evaluation of the process. Such deadlines are not only necessary to keep the process going, but also have a positive influence on the support for the co-creation process among stakeholders and key players.[11]

6.   How to prevent priority shifting?

All too often, an enthusiastic team develops a concept, only to abandon it because other projects have been prioritized. People – and organizations, too – are prone to getting distracted by urgent things. Unfortunately, the co-creation of new solutions is often not considered urgent, especially not when an organization has limited resources to invest in innovation. Although most urgent things seldom create value on the longer term, they can very pressing on the short term. As a result, people and means that were originally allocated to a co-creation trajectory, may get replaced to the urgent matter.

Postponing leads to quitting

Shifting priorities may be the most important reason that co-creation often does not lead to implementation. Although in general the idea is that the co-creation process will get re-fueled when the urgent matter has been dealt with, in reality this seldom happens. Often, time will pass the concept: a competitor may have introduced something similar in the meantime, or market changes may have made the conceptual solution redundant. Possibly, the urgent matter has used all available funds, which may cause the co-creation process to stay on pause until new funds are available.

Insurance company ignored the target group "wealthy seniors" after all

More and more organizations are focused on developing scenarios and strategies in response to the quick aging of western societies. In 2014 a European insurance company decided to start a co-creation trajectory with the target group 'wealthy seniors'. This should lead to 1) a deep understanding of the needs and wishes of this target group with respect to finance and insurance, and 2) a dedicated approach for this group, possibly with specific products or product packages. The enthusiastic employee assigned to this project first conducted a comprehensive customer-insight-trajectory, including an elaborate desk research. The next step would be to have a substantial group of wealthy seniors spend a day with internal and external experts, working in subgroups on the development of ideas following from the insights yielded by the research. However, just when the participants were to be invited, the project manager was assigned to another (very urgent) project, and an insecure intern took over. He kept doing more and more research, until ultimately the insurance company decided to abandon the project altogether.

Allocating the Co-creator to another project may mean that he or she won't be available anymore by the time the co-creation trajectory gets picked up again. Simply appointing a different Co-creator is tricky, because the new person does not share the understanding of the market and target group that gave rise to the conceptual solution, and thus may not 'own' it. More often than not, a new Co-creator will loop back to the research phase, and is likely to deliver an entirely new concept, based on new insights.

An innovative education method was never brought to market

In co-creation with students, teachers, and principals of various schools, an educational publisher developed a concept for an innovative method for vocational education. The concept was in a far stage of development, and had gotten good scores from user tests. It was being developed by an inspired project manager who had her own team, plenty of financial means, and a lot of decision making power. Then the 2008 financial crisis hit. Like many organizations, this publisher, too, pulled the plug from most innovation projects and returned to the core business. When the project manager was assigned a different project, she started to look for other challenges outside of the organization. By the time the publisher put innovation back on its calendar, she had left the company.

Finally, postponing a co-creation process carries the risk that in the meantime, enthusiastic stakeholders make place for new skeptics that do not believe in the development of the conceptual solution. They have not been part of the co-creation process, and may have other priorities. Staying on track is the only remedy!

Solidifying the term and parameters for evaluation

To keep a co-creation trajectory going, also in the face of other urgent challenges, it is smart to 'officially' allocate the Co-creator for a specified term. To do this, the initiating organization and the Co-creator should sign a contract, specifying the duration of the trajectory, as well as the parameters for evaluation. When the Co-creator is an external party (for instance a contractor or detached consultant), part of the payment may be subject to the output. When the Co-creator is an internal party, a bonus may be attached to the output. This will motivate the Co-creator to guide the trajectory up to the point of implementation.

Ideally, the Co-creator (not the initiating organization) will propose the parameters central to evaluation of the co-creation trajectory's output. Bear in mind that result parameters are more objective than process parameters and directly related to the solution's performance in real life. With process parameters describing how the process went and to what extent the rules and procedures of the initial organizations were met, result parameters describe what outcomes have been established. The relevance of various possible result parameters – for instance sales and visitor numbers or product reviews – depends on the challenge and solution.

7. Questions to our readers

1. Have you ever been part of a co-creation process that did not lead to implementation?

2. How do you score on the profile of the ideal Co-creator?
a. What would be your strong points as a Co-creator?
b. In what respect would you need external support, education or training?

3. How easy or hard would it be for a Co-creator to realize sufficient time, resources, and decision making power within your organization? What are the biggest challenges in doing this?

Principle 4: Productive.
Complete co-creation leads
to implementation of the
co-created solution.

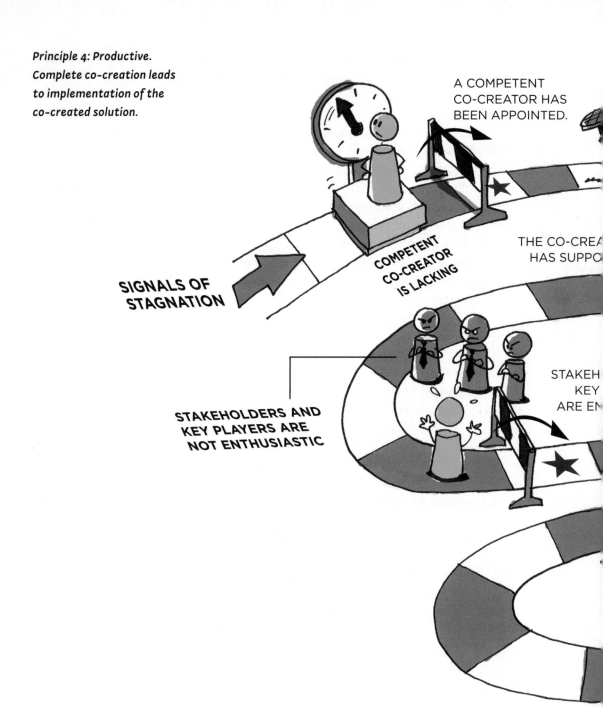

A COMPETENT
CO-CREATOR HAS
BEEN APPOINTED.

THE CO-CREA
HAS SUPPO

COMPETENT
CO-CREATOR
IS LACKING

SIGNALS OF
STAGNATION

STAKEH
KEY
ARE EN

STAKEHOLDERS AND
KEY PLAYERS ARE
NOT ENTHUSIASTIC

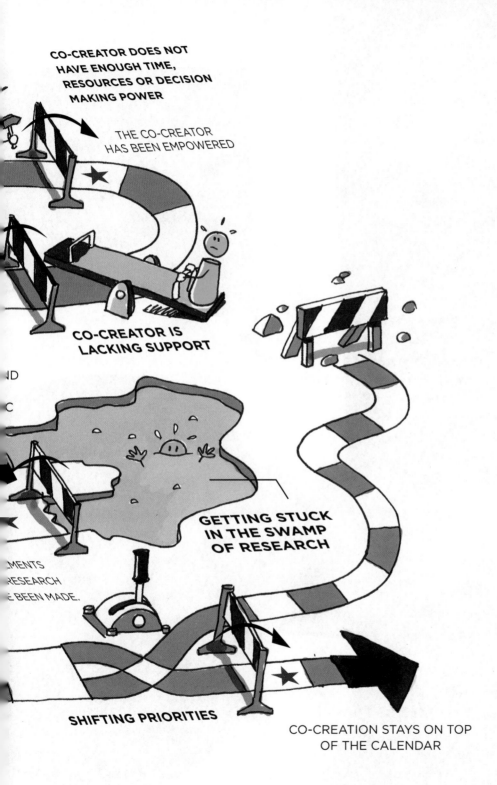

CO-CREATOR DOES NOT HAVE ENOUGH TIME, RESOURCES OR DECISION MAKING POWER

THE CO-CREATOR HAS BEEN EMPOWERED

CO-CREATOR IS LACKING SUPPORT

ND

C

GETTING STUCK IN THE SWAMP OF RESEARCH

MENTS
RESEARCH
E BEEN MADE.

SHIFTING PRIORITIES

CO-CREATION STAYS ON TOP OF THE CALENDAR

In complete
co-creation,
relevant information
is accessible to all
participants.

PRINCIPLE 5
TRANSPARENT

For a long time, so-called 'black box procedures' were the norm.
It was a fully acceptable practice to identify a business issue, hire an
agency, and wait for them to deliver a solution. However, the key shift
driving the transition from the Power Paradigm to the Co-creation
Paradigm is the progressive opening up of organizations.[1] This reflects
both an intensifying internal motivation, as well as an increasing
external pressure to be honest and transparent about organizational
procedures and decision making processes.

Organizations often follow a 'black box procedure' when developing solutions. That roughly goes like this: a group of people is asked to deliver a solution for a certain challenge. After some time (and money) has been spent, the group does deliver a solution, but are not clear how exactly they got there. In other words, the process from assignment to outcome is a black box. For organizations to play along in the co-creation paradigm, they have to be willing to leave the black box behind and embrace transparency. This includes open knowledge sharing, collaborative insight development, and a shared view of organizational processes.

CASE 48

Blendhub Corporation fights the black box in the food powder chain[3]

Inspired by the world food crisis, the Spanish business-to-business organization Blendhub Corporation, led by the Dane Henrik Stamm Kristensen, has taken on the challenge to realize change in the agrifood value chain. From the wish to give more people at more locations in the world access to honest and safe foods, Blendhub made her processes entirely transparent. In an interview with TheCoCreators, Kristensen explains: "Ninety percent of the food in the world is produced by industries that are structurally lacking in knowledge and means with respect to food technology, and that are entirely dependent on external suppliers of rough materials, blended food powders, and processing technology." He goes on: "The food powder chain has long been characterized by a strained relationship between food manufacturers and suppliers of rough ingredients and blends. Manufacturers of end-products want to know how these blends have been prepared, what ingredients they contain, and what the related costs are. They tend to only get a short, often incomplete and sometimes even incorrect technical specification. This makes quality control and safety checking of end-products difficult, the price unclear, and hampers healthy competition. Moreover, when a blend has been approved of by the manufacturer, it is extremely hard or even impossible to change suppliers, which leads to a co-dependent relationship. In the end, the consumer is the victim of this dynamic." Breaking with the tradition of obscurity in the category, Blendhub Corporation develops its SMART powder blends in complete transparency. Kristensen: "This way we are adding to the production of safe and honest foods for end-users!"

1.   The introduction to this book, as well as principle 7 (value-driven) deal with the power- versus co-creation paradigm.

The popular Dutch marketing and trendwatching blog FrankWatching.com calls transparency an important trend that will continue.[4] Over a short period of time, it has developed from *'having nothing to hide'* to *'spontaneously showing and proofing that there is nothing to hide'*.[5] When organizations decide to embark on this trend, they are rewarded by their end-users. For instance, 69% of the American consumers prefer buying something from a brand that is proactively open about its objectives and results with respect to corporate social responsibility.[6]

Reading guide for principle 5 – transparent

In this chapter we aim to answer the following two questions:

1. Why is the black box a structural misfit with complete co-creation?
2. How does transparency relate to complete co-creation?

As usual we will start the chapter with the case JIP Noord, and end it with three questions to our readers.

CASE 49

Transparency in developing JIP Noord[7]

During the development of JIP Noord the Co-creator used various channels to keep all involved parties up-to-date. She organized frequent co-creation group meetings, sent regular informational emails to other involved parties, and used workshops, email, WhatsApp, text messaging, and Facebook to keep youth as intended user group informed and actively involved. This way, all participants in the co-creation trajectory always knew in which phase they were, what the status was of the decision making process, and also – as soon as this was clear – what the available budget was. The Co-creator documented all decisions, choices, and next steps – as far as possible traced back to what end-users and partner organizations perceived as added value. During the trajectory she organized a few smaller meetings with decision makers, as well as several larger ones with all directly and indirectly involved parties. During these meetings youth and other members of the

2.   From: Spinoza, B. (1673) *Tractacus Politicus*. Rendered in HTML and text by Jon Roland, The Constitution Society (1998)

3.   More information about Blendhub: http://bit.ly/2xDFrCQ

4.   More information about the popularity of transparency can be found in the trend research by CommunicatiePanel (2015) · http://bit.ly/2xEaxKD

5.   More information and numbers about transparency as a trend can be found here: http://bit.ly/2wuyzCU

6.   Cone Communications, October 2012: Cone Communications Corporate Social Return Trend Tracker http://bit.ly/2jtol4a

7.   Background information about this case can be found in the introduction to this book.

co-creation group presented their ideas and answered questions from the attendees. In addition, members of the co-creation group visited several JIP's and JSP's (youth service points) in and around Amsterdam, and youth accompanied the alderman and other interested people from the city quarter and potential partner organizations on a visit to the successful JIP in The Hague.

Thus, the final concept for JIP Noord did not come from a black box, but resulted from an open process which was widely supported by the city quarter, potential partner organizations, and the future end-users. While youth in similar trajectories tend to quit because they are ignored for too long or only informed of crucial decisions after the fact, youth involved in the development of JIP Noord stayed loyal (and actually increased in numbers during the process), also when the decision making took much longer than expected. Because they were informed about the political background of the delay and adaptations of the original plans, they were able to understand and accept. They felt taken seriously, and kept their faith that JIP Noord would become a reality.

The same was true for the potential partners. There was a real risk that they would abandon the development process as a result of the delay and changing vantage points. However, by continuously inviting them for meetings, asking for their input, and keeping them informed about the project status, they stayed interested and divided the consultancy hours at JIP Noord long before the location opened its doors.

1.   Why is the black box a structural misfit with complete co-creation?

The result of a process that is not open to all involved parties may come across convincing and innovative, and may promise exactly what the initiating organization wants to hear. However, at the same time it may cause insecurity among those that were kept outside of it. When people feel excluded, they tend to ask questions. Why were certain choices made? Which assumptions were guiding? What steps have been followed? What alternative solutions were rejected and why? When such questions are not being answered, filling in based on assumptions will occur, and trust in the trajectory may dissolve.

Clinging to the black box

For many organizations, closed procedures have become the norm over time, often even documented as such in a (non-optional) procedure. These organizations may not be aware of the benefits of transparency. They may also not feel ready for more openness, possibly even being afraid of it. Fear of competitors 'stealing' information and ideas, as well as fear of losing control of the creative process may play a role. Finally, closed organizations may simply lack the needed knowledge and experience with transparency to feel secure adopting it.[8]

8.   Barriers against adopting transparancy parallel barriers against adopting complete co-creatie as introduced in the introduction of this book. Principle 6 (supported) deals with overcoming barriers against adopting complete co-creation.

9.   In Widrich, L. (2013). FastCompany blogpost: http://bit.ly/2fonc9P

> 💬 *To us, transparency isn't a buzzword. It's a huge competitive advantage when everyone knows what everyone is working on and getting done. It seems obvious, right? But I'm constantly shocked by how many companies say they understand the importance of transparency but don't take any steps to make their companies more transparent."* Leo Widrich, Founder of Buffer[9]

Even when an organization is fully committed to adopt transparency, it may still end up with a black box procedure as a result from hiring an external party that works that way, such as a consultancy firm, an innovation agency, a research agency, or a creative agency – that works that way. Even agencies claiming to work in co-creation with end-users tend to integrate 'black box moments' in their processes. Announced or unannounced, they may conduct (part of) their creative or analytical process behind closed doors, sometimes presenting the result as a product of co-creation. This is usually related to the fear that allowing clients, end-users, and other relevant parties to take part in their process, will disturb it.

Risks of the black box

The not knowing and insecurity evoked by a black box procedure oppose the needs for insight and control that the initiating organization and all other involved parties generally have. Insight and control are not only necessary for participants to feel taken seriously, but also for sensible decision making that will yield positive outcomes on on both the short and longer term.

Even if a black box procedure may initially leads to a successful introduction, it is a suboptimal way of working, because an understanding of the keys to success exists only among those that were part of the process. Knowledge of crucial information disappears the moment these people are no longer accessible or for some reason decide to not share their understanding.

> 💬 *The result was a concept I liked. That is, I could imagine this becoming a succes. But because we were not involved in its development, we didn't know how to execute it."*
> Designer at an international food concern

Whatever the reasons for holding on to the black box may be, organizations striving to be successful in the co-creation paradigm will need to let it go. Closed processes can't co-exist with openness, one of the three core values of this paradigm.[10]

2. How does transparency relate to complete co-creation?

Transparency in a process of complete co-creation means that all internal and external participants share and interpret the relevant information and insights together, and that none of the involved parties are keeping a hidden agenda. This open sharing of information will happen via various channels – from live meetings to online and mobile apps[11] – and includes both content-related information and process-related information. At the start of the trajectory, it needs to be clear how team members will communicate with one another, and how information will be shared and stored.

Asana, a solution for transparency in teams[12]

Start-ups are capitalizing on the trend of open knowledge sharing with online tools for collaboration and the sharing of information within teams. A successful example is Asana, a task management tool developed by Dustin Moskovitz (co-founder of Facebook) and Justin Rosenstein (ex-Facebook and ex-Google). Asana is a web-based and mobile tool providing teams with the possibility to share their work in an open and structured way, without a cluttered email inbox and unnecessary team meetings. Transparency in communication is crucial for Asana; they call this "transparency till it hurts". Asana's co-workers can share, plan, and organize tasks and information, and follow each other's work. They can also give direct feedback to each other's ideas and conduct online brainstorms. According to Rosenstein this is not about knowing everything about everyone, but giving everybody access to all information they may need to be effective in their work. Asana was founded in 2008, and is currently being used by large organizations, such as Spotify and Foursquare.

Transparency with respect to content

Content-related transparency is about sharing facts and insights necessary to understand the challenge, such as up-to-date information about relevant laws and trends in the market, background information about the target group, market and competitor analyses, personas, customer journeys, reports from customer insight trajectories, and other research reports. It is a good idea to make an online, readily accessible knowledge center to store this type of information so that everyone can find it and build on it.

Transparency with respect to the process

Process-related transparency means that at any given time, the co-creation team has access to up-to-date and complete information about the process. For the most part, this will be practical information dealing with plannings, tasks, and responsibilities, but it may also include subjective information about participants' perceptions the process.

Practical information

Practical information includes notes from meetings, lists of decisions made, timelines, to do lists, calendars and agendas for meetings and events etc. It may also entail agreements and contracts with respect to tasks, time investment, ownership of content and ideas, secrecy etc. There are various apps that make this type of information sharing easy.

CASE 51

Transparency as a key part of co-creating adidas GLITCH[13]

In 2015, the adidas Global Football business unit worked on a new product innovation that re-imagined the football boot (or soccer cleat) as two separate and unique components – an inner sock and an outer skin. The boot's socks and skins were interchangeable, allowing consumers to switch their looks and boot performance on-demand.

To create this innovative experience, the adidas project team, including of 20+ members from Strategy, Product Development, Design, eCommerce and Marketing, used the collaboration platform Batterii to co-create with consumers. The transparent approach did not only help keeping team members informed, but also rallied everyone around the consumer insights and overall experience to deliver.

In an interview with TheCoCreators, Chad Reynolds, founder of Batterii, explains: "Transparency helps to make better decisions. Using Missions (time-allotted requests to capture content into a room inside of Batterii) is a scalable method to gather authentic insights from consumers in their native environments and real situations. This allowed adidas team members to see first-hand, using the actual assets in leadership meetings to affect decision making. Also, Batterii provided adidas teams and consumers with one place to collaborate. This allowed research and insights to sit next to ideas and strategy. The process was fluid and organic, and the quality of information and insights gathered improved as the team evolved their thinking."

In November 2016, adidas GLITCH launched exclusively in the UK. The consumers who participated in the co-creation experience were on full display inside of the app and were mentioned in communications and through social media posts. Using insights from multiple engagements along the process, the adidas team was able to improve every customer touchpoint in a fast, authentic and meaningful way. After only six months in the market, GLITCH had been so successful that Berlin was selected as the second city to launch, with plans to expand across the globe.

---

10.   The other two core values of the co-creation paradigm are sharing and collaborating. The co-creation paradigm was introduced in the introduction of this book. Principle 7 (value-driven) elaborates on it.

11.   Principles 3 (onging), 4 (productive), and 6 (supported) deal with various ways of sharing and filing information.

12.   More information about Asana can be found here: https://asana.com and here http://bit.ly/2f02OuV

13.   More information about adidas GLITCH: www.adidas.com/us/glitch and Batterii: www.batterii.com

Left: consumer completes mobile mission with Batterii; right: the online GLITCH platform

Clarity about tasks and responsibilities

From the beginning, the Co-creator will position himself as the one with the overview, as well as the one filling in the practical and political prerequisites for successful co-creation. He will presents an overview of things that have been taken care of, such as support for the challenge and co-creation process among stakeholders and key players, a deep understanding of the end-users, a powerful key insight, a shared project folder in the cloud, and a closed group on a social media platform such as WhatsApp, Facebook, Yammer or Slack.

In addition, he will indicate how he, ideally supported by his assistant, will take care of the practical and political prerequisites and resources during the creative process. Think arranging meeting locations and catering, information sharing, feeding ongoing support for co-creation in the top, securing a sufficient budget, creating and maintaining an online panel with end-users and other involved parties, the recruitment of new end-users and connecting directly and indirectly involved parties and experts when necessary.

Finally, the Co-creator will initiate a discussion about the expected input of the other participants: who does what when. This depends on the group he is sharing expectations with: members of co-creation team and opportunity work groups are expected to contribute more frequently and more substantially, than members of the advisory council. It is important for the Co-creator not to assign tasks to people, but to have people verbalize their own ambitions and promises. The Co-creator will integrate all of this in a project plan, which will be an important tool for the management of expectations throughout the co-creation process.[14]

14. Principe 3 (ongoing) deals with the project plan.

15. More information about Wikipedia can be found here: www.wikipedia.org and here: http://bit.ly/2xEoWGr

Sharing experiences in the co-creation team

In the co-creation team, process-related transparency should involve the sharing of experiences during the adventure of complete co-creation. For this to occur, the team dynamics must feel safe enough for participants to share their feelings and experiences, both as team members and as participants in the larger co-creation process. Team members should also feel comfortable giving each other feedback on their delivered work and functioning in the team.

Benefits of transparency

Transparency in complete co-creation has a positive effect on both the quality of the developed solution, as well as the atmosphere within the co-creation team and the collaboration with parties outside of it. Thus, it will deliver at least four important benefits.

Benefit 1: insight

The choice for an open platform, where participants from inside and outside of the initiating organization can share all relevant findings, will allow the co-creation team to weigh, support, enrich, and interpret from various relevant points of view. This will lead to adding more – also less obvious – information, as well as to a shared evolving understanding. An open process does not leave any space for opposing interpretations, since everyone is always working from the same vantage points.

CASE 52

Wikipedia, icon of open knowledge sharing

Wikipedia, the world's largest and most popular online encyclopedia is one of today's most transparent organizations and a trendsetter in the field of open knowledge sharing. Wikipedia is the continuous evolving outcome of an ongoing collective collaboration between international author-volunteers, who have produced more than thirty billion articles in 286 languages about a wide variety of subjects pertaining to humanity's history. The power behind its success is the free accessibility of all knowledge and information that the billions of volunteers have filled the site's knowledge data bank with since the site's founding in 2001. Anyone is allowed to add, adapt, and correct articles. The founder of the organization, Jimmy Wales, describes this as such: "Imagine a world in which every human being is free to share in the sum of all knowledge." Wikipedia shows how far co-creation may reach. However, as trendsetter the organization also meets problems that haven't been met before. For instance, the open knowledge platform is currently dealing with an unexpected loss of volunteers due to chaotic procedures and bureaucracy.[15]

Benefit 2: clarity

An open, well documented co-creation process creates clarity for internal and external participants, stakeholders, and key players. Steps taken and planned are known, decisions traceable, and everyone knows in which phase the process is. Moreover, because the roles of all participants are clear to everyone, the process will unfold smoothly and efficient. There is no overlap between team members' activities, nor are they deviating from the team's mission. In addition, this clarity makes it easy to seek connection to other parties. External parties (e.g. agencies, suppliers, etc.) can add to the process in an efficient and focused way, because their assignment is unambiguous and they know exactly where in the process their added value is needed.

Benefit 3: involvement

Organizations that choose to conduct an open co-creation process will inspire the participants to give their most and will realize a high level of involvement and support among participants from inside and outside of the organization. Participants will own any solution that results from an open process in which they have fulfilled a role. As opposed to receiving a ready-to-implement solution from a black box, having been part of a successful creative process will evoke a sense of pride. Not just pride about the co-created solution, but also about the organization that made it possible.

Furthermore, an open team process does not leave any space for inequality of team members' efforts, since everyone's input is clearly visible for all. Furthermore, no-one needs to struggle alone with potential obstacles; the team will conquer these in collaboration, because everyone knows and recognizes them.

Benefit 4: trust

Just like closedness creating distrust, openness leads to trust. Of course there is always the risk of trust to be taken advantage of, but this does not outweigh the huge benefits of an open process. When the participants trust one another, as well as the process, support for the outcomes will follow automatically. This makes implementation easier, especially when stakeholders and key players have been part of the process.

When a party is with-holding information, the best case scenario is a suboptimal co-creation outcome. Worst case is a breach of trust, delusion of the other parties, stagnation of the collaboration, and potentially negative messages leaking about the party with-holding the information, usually the initiating organization. After all, the consumer credo holds: "*When an organization behaves secretive, they have secrets.*"

The curious case of the unidentifiable duck[16]

In 2011 the Dutch critical TV-program De Keuringsdienst van Waarde ("the Inspection Service of Value") conducted a documented research into Oscillococcinum, a hard to pronounce homeopathic remedy against the flu. The active ingredient is, according to the packaging 'Anas Barbariae hepatis et cordis extractum'. This is Latin for the heart and liver of the musk duck. This ingredient inspired the reporters of the Keuringsdienst to find out more. Their research led them to a factory in France. After repeated requests, the researchers were admitted to the factory, but they were not allowed to talk about how the production processes. All questions pertaining to this – for instance where the ducks were – were answered with the remark that the production process can't be discussed because it is protected.

An objective analysis of the remedy showed that the heart and liver of the ducks is not traceable in the remedy, which mainly consists of lactose.

Upset consumers placed comments on the website of the Keuringsdienst and voiced their distrust via various social media: "With this secrecy they make themselves very suspicious." And: "I think it doesn't contain any duck at all, and that it is just a fable. Otherwise that manufacturer wouldn't act so secretive about the recipe."

Potential boundaries of transparency

Transparency in a process of complete co-creation does not mean that the initiating organization needs to make all of its sensitive information accessible to everyone.
It pertains only to the information that is relevant in the co-creation process. And even then, it may be smart to consciously share certain information later in the process – for instance about the (im)possibility of specific production processes or budgets – so as to not hamper it by highlighting potential obstacles. Moreover, in order to give the process a new impulse or prevent the participants from abandoning the original assignment, the Co-creator can consciously control the information stream or direct the focus to certain bits of information.

In any co-creation process, opportunity work groups will regularly get together to work on certain aspects of the trajectory or take strategic decisions amongst themselves. That, too, agrees with transparency, as long as these work groups will share their insights and decisions with the other participants at some point in the co-creation process.[17]

16.   The episode of de Keuringsdienst van Waarde about Oscillococcinum can be watched here http://bit.ly/2wg8pbL

17.   Principles 1 (together), 3 (ongoing), and 6 (supported) deal with the consistency and function of the various work groups.

Publicity as a form of transparency

Seeking publicity is a way of showing the world that there is nothing to hide, while at the same time raising interest and support for the co-creation endeavor. If allowed by all participants, it is a good adiea to ask (local) media to cover key steps throughout the process. Press may be present at the kick-off session, research presentation, concept presentation, and launch of the solution. In order to make sure that the effects of media exposure will be positive, it is wise for people facing the media to practice what to share and how.

Radical transparency as a characteristic of co-creative organizations

The four benefits of transparency in a co-creation process can have profound effects when openness becomes a guiding organizational principle. This is referred to as 'radical transparency'. More and more organizations, including a relatively large number of startups, embrace it. Examples are Seventh Generation, manufacturer of environmentally friendly household products, online music service Spotify, outdoor brand Patagonia, and Moz, a developer of SEO software and digital marketing tools.

> We [Seventh Generation] have built a level of authenticity and transparency that we believe is one of the key reasons behind the loyalty we have from our consumers. Radical transparency I believe is a critical hallmark of a company that is going to be sustainable. [...] You cannot judge yourself to be sustainable or responsible. You can only be judged by others."
> Jeffrey Hollender, Co-founder and CEO of Seventh Generation[18]

> I honestly believe that if Redfin were stripped absolutely bare for all the world to see, naked and humiliated in the sunlight, more people would do business with us."
> Glenn Kelman, CEO at Redfin[19]

> We are always able to speak up and provide suggestions to the company regarding day-to-day activities, and work issues. We are always asked for our opinions and ideas. Suggestions are always taken into consideration. Everyone is offered to have their own voice to speak up. Team members are always encouraged to provide their ideas. We have a special group that compiles ideas, and passes them along for consideration. I am very proud to work for this company. We are treated with respect, and provided with the tools to succeed in our work day."
> Zappos employee[20]

> **❝** *Of all the factors that contribute to more agile software releases, our own experience has taught us that transparency and communication make all the difference."*
> Dalibor Siroky, Co-founder and Co-CEO of Plutora.[21]

Research links radical transparency to organizational success.[22] Naturally, an organization with a lot of knowledge and understanding, unequivocal processes, motivated and involved employees, and trusted by its end-users can count on the loyalty of existing good employees and clients. Moreover, such an organization will work as a magnet for new good personnel and new end-users.

CASE 54

Happy employees at Zappos realize an amazing customer service

Online retailer Zappos wants to deliver exceptionally good customer service. Its core value is: "Build Open and Honest Relationships with Communication." Internally, as well as externally, Zappos has an open culture. This includes free company tours for anyone interested, Q and A sessions between clients and managers, the website Zapposinsight.com which offers full insight of the organizational culture, and the live streaming of all quarterly meetings, including presentations by the CEO. Zappos employees function as equal co-workers. In 2014 this resulted in the establishment of a Holocracy, in which all titles and hierarchy have been eliminated.[23]

Fear of sharing negative characteristics still prevents many organizations from following the pioneers of the radical transparency movement. That this is something that need not be feared is illustrated by the increase in customer trust and loyalty after Seventh Generation openly shared all negative aspects of its products – from mistakes in the packaging to 'wrong' ingredients.[24] Research by Tapscott & Ticoll confirms that transparency – including the sharing of negative information – is the best way to build a trustworthy reputation.[25]

18.   Quote from a presentation on HSM's World Innovation Forum (2010): http://bit.ly/2f07jMv

19.   In: Thompson, C. (2007) *The See-Through CEO*. Wired Magazine, issue 15.04. Redfin is a real estate agency. More information can be found here: http://bit.ly/2x0TB0f

20.   Quote from own qualitative research.

21.   Quote posted at the following blog: http://bit.ly/2x4ARue

22.   More information can be found here: Warren, B., Goleman, D. & O'Toole, J. (2008). *Transparency: Creating a Culture of Candor*. Jossey-Bass, San Francisco. This book quotes a 2005 research showing that a group of 27 'most transparent' American organizations beat the S&P 500 with 11.3%. More information on the benefits of transparency can be found here: http://bit.ly/2xEyHVq

Buffer, a radically transparent social media start-up[26]

At first sight a social-media-start-up like any other, Buffer was founded in 2010. The service offers a smart way to manage social media. Special about Buffer is that the founders, Leo Widrich and Joel Gascoigne, made the start-up fully transparent right from the start. For instance, every employee knows exactly how much all existing and future colleagues are earning or will earn. Salaries follow from a formula, and special deals are not allowed. Moreover, all communication is accessible to all employees, and there is a practice of daily sharing the progress and lessons learned. Buffer even goes so far as to give every new employee a Jawbone UP, a wrist band that monitors sleep, movement, and other parameters of health. This lead to co-workers openly discussing their wellbeing, for instance why they aren't getting enough sleep. According to Buffer this form of radical transparency has a very positive effect on the collaboration, trust, and personal growth within its teams.

Co-creative organizations naturally embrace radical transparency. With their mission to add sustainable value for the end-users, their own organization, their business partners, and ultimately the entire planet, they have nothing to hide. On the contrary, they believe that the open sharing of all relevant information will help adding even more value!

3. Questions to our readers

1. What are your experiences with working in an open versus a closed environment?

2. Did you ever have to deal with a black box? If so, what were its effects on you and other involved people?

3. What might be barriers to the building of a transparent co-creation environment in your organization? How might these be overcome?

---

23. More information about Zappos can be found here: http://bit.ly/2wuOVv6 and here: http://bit.ly/2weInFT

24. More information about Seventh Generation can be found here: http://bit.ly/2fo7JMv and here: http://www.seventhgeneration.com

25. Tapscott, D. & Ticoll, D. (2003). *The naked corporation: How the age of transparency will revolutionize business.* New York: The Free Press.

26. More information about Buffer can be found here: http://bit.ly/2fonc9P

Principle 5: Transparent.
In complete co-creation, relevant information
is accessible to all participants.

TRANSPARENCY AVENUE

BLACK BOX

Potential consequences of the black box:
• insecurity
• suspicion

Potential causes of the black box:
• Habituation
• Fear of competitors
• Fear of control
• Fear of disturbing the creative process
• Lack of experience with transparency

BLACK BOX COURT

Benefits of transparency:
• Insight
• Clarity
• Involvement
• Trust

• **Content-related information**
• **Process-related information**

Complete

co-creation is

supported by all

involved parties.

PRINCIPLE 6
SUPPORTED

In a supported co-creation process, all involved parties understand
the challenge and view it as important, believe in complete co-creation
as the way to tackle it, and are motivated to contribute personal
strengths, skills, and knowledge to the development of a solution.
This can be a rather large contribution, as in active participation
throughout the process. It can also be smaller, but nonetheless
crucial, for instance creating a favorable political climate.

We can't stress the importance of establishing and maintaining support enough! When there is a lack of support among stakeholders, key players, and the co-creation team, the co-creation endeavor is certain to fail.[1] This is why 'political antenna', 'social skills', and 'networking skills' rank among the top needed competencies of the Co-creator. Throughout the process, he will spend much of his time doing everything he can, to create and maintain support. This chapter is dedicated to these support-enhancing actions.
They are summarized in the table below.

Support-enhancing actions in a process of complete co-creation

SUPPORT-ENHANCING ACTIVITIES	BARRIER-OVERCOMING ACTIVITIES
* Pitching challenge and approach * Highlighting benefits and sharing best practices * Organizing large-scale, interactive sessions * Installing a multidisciplinary advisory council * Facilitating shared research experiences * Sharing decision making processes * Continuous communication about the process * Making and sharing an implementation plan * Giving compliments and rewards * Highlighting the puzzle principle * Organizing monitoring sessions after launch	* Comparing the budget of a complete co-creation trajectory with the realistic budget of a standard development trajectory * Cutting the co-creation trajectory into pieces to try getting a go per piece * Making tangible what complete co-creation takes in terms of capacity (FTE's) * Comparing the duration of a complete co-creation with a standard development trajectory * Planning ahead what can be planned * Positioning the co-creation trajectory as a semi-independent start-up * Pitching a phased planning * Having stakeholders and key players experience a creative process with end-users first-hand * Conducting co-creation experiments to make people acquainted with the phenomenon in a safe setting * Accepting the voice-of-customer-model whilst working on preparing the organization for complete co-creation * Establishing a safe atmosphere for an open dialogue between participants in which they can freely share their stakes and commit to a common goal * Starting a co-creation trajectory with a signed manifesto in which all participants agree with the shared goal

1. Principle 1 (together) describes the concepts of stakeholders, key players, and the co-creation team.

Support touches on other principles of complete co-creation. It is, for instance, closely tied to the prerequisites of productive collaboration, an important one being intrinsic motivation.[2] Furthermore, support will only flow from a productive, transparent process.[3] For these things, a competent Co-creator is crucial.[4]

Reading guide principle 6 – supported

The Co-creator will have to be an expert in promoting support and helping overcome barriers against it. This chapter gives guidelines for accomplishing this, answering two main questions:

1. How to promote support for complete co-creation?
2. How to overcome barriers against supporting complete co-creation?

As usual, we will start this chapter with the case JIP Noord and complete it with three questions to our readers.

CASE 56

Support among directly and indirectly involved parties during the development of JIP Noord[5]

Because the various parties felt taken seriously in the development process and saw their input integrated in the developing JIP, everyone perceived JIP Noord as partly 'theirs'. This showed not only in the responsible alderman's enthusiasm in publicly sharing the success, but also in spontaneous contributions from youth and other involved parties, without expecting a tangible reward. Moreover, several stakeholders were interested to run JIP Noord or at least stay actively involved by conducting live consults with youth at JIP Noord's location. Finally, partner organizations were willing to train interns working at JIP Noord.

1. How to promote support for complete co-creation?

A strong start is half the work! Creating support should start even before embarking on a co-creation trajectory. During the co-creation process and also after implementation of the solution, maintaining support among all directly and indirectly involved parties remains one of the Co-creator's most important tasks. To do this, he can engage in various support-enhancing activities, starting with pitching the challenge and complete co-creation among the decision makers.

2. Principle 1 (together) lists the prerequisites for productive collaboration.

3. Principle 5 (transparant) describes the importance of an open process.

Pitching the challenge and the approach

The pitch of the challenge and complete co-creation as the process to tackle it may happen in a group session. However, if time allows, individual meetings with stakeholders are best. Regardless of the setting, observing and listening very carefully is crucial. The goal is to define each stakeholder's dreams and fears. A deep understanding of drivers and barriers will help create a clear image of 'what's in it for me' for everyone.

It is possible for a stakeholder to recognize the challenge and to admit that it is important, yet lack a genuine interest in solving it. Only a politically sensitive Co-creator will recognize that. Asking every stakeholder how much money, time, capacity, and other resources they are willing to invest in a co-creation trajectory to solve the challenge at hand, may help to make commitment (or the lack thereof) tangible. In order to recognize and overcome resistance, it is wise for the Co-creator to prepare well for the most important barriers against co-creation.[6]

> 66 *For some of the potential partners in JIP Noord, the intitial motivation to participate seemed to be primarily inspired by the fear that something would be conjured up threatening the existence of their own organization. However, as the process unfolded, participants' enthusiasm about what we were doing together grew. They started to look beyond their own organization – namely at the relevance of JIP Noord for the local youth."*
> Martine Jansen, former Co-creator JIP Noord

Usually, it works well in a pitch to present some statistics on the market and target group that show the relevance of the challenge. For this, a quick desk research suffices. In addition, end-user quotes about the challenge may be gathered by means of a brief online survey or street research.[7] Movie clips of end-users talking about the challenge add convincing power.

Highlighting benefits and sharing best practices

Highlighting the benefits of complete co-creation and presenting examples of successful organizations that work according to its principles, tends to have a positive effect on support. This is not only good to do during the pitch and kick-off session, but should be done regularly throughout the co-creation process. Best practices may be presented according to the five benefits of complete co-creation, as done below for telecom provider *bliep.

---

4.   Principle 4 (productive) deals with the implementation of outcomes and the role of the Co-creator.

5.   More information about this case can be found in the introduction of this book.

The five benefits of complete co-creation as illustrated by the case *bliep

Relevance
When the intended end-user group is consistently involved in all the necessary steps in a development process, the output will be relevant, recognizable, and attractive for this group.

Before the youth-focused telecom provider *bliep changed ownership in 2015, youth as end-users played a continuous role in the company. Its head quarters in the center of Amsterdam were always filled with the chatter of young voices. Youth ran the helpdesk, co-developed new products, services, and communication – they were even members of the management team! Co-founder Jochem Wieringa explains: "We saw this as the only way to be successful among a target group that is characterized by a deeply rooted suspicion against our industry. The co-creation with youth – and also sometimes with their parents – led to ideas we would have never thought of ourselves. For instance the 'share your credit button'. That was an idea from a girl who was struggling with running out of credit at times, and came up with this idea to be able to borrow some from friends."

Marketing
The involved end-users will spread word among their peers about the development process long before it yields a solution. This will give the market introduction a boost. Moreover, in a complete co-creation process, end-users play an active role in developing marketing instruments, thus increasing their effectiveness. Finally, claiming end-user involvement can increase the credibility of the co-created solution's benefits.

The intensive involvement of youth in the product development of *bliep caused it to be widely known among the target group long before the market launch in 2012. Shortly after launch, *bliep had already sold twice as many SIM-cards as the most optimistic estimation. Until the change of ownership, *bliep ranked steadily among the top 3 of best selling prepaid brands in the Dutch telecomretail. Most telecom companies grow by relying heavily on advertising in traditional mass media or by surpassing competitors in the incentives for telecom stores selling their products. In contrast, *bliep never spent a cent for traditional advertising and structurally paid retailers less than the competitors.
Instead, the brand followed its target group's advice and invested in viral marketing. Wieringa: "Some of our youth had contacts with influential Youtubers. They asked these Youtubers to make content featuring *bliep indirectly. In exchange we financed the production of those movie clips, allowing them to have a much higher quality than normally. Because the target group had taken the initiative and speaks the language of their peers, the movies instantly hit the right chord."

6.   Overcoming barriers against complete co-creation is discussed later in this chapter. Principle 4 (productive) deals

7.   Quick research in the founding phase was briefly mentioned in principle 3 (ongoing). Principle 2 (with end-users) gives more information about the different research tools.

Motivation

From the very beginning it is evident to everyone involved why, for whom, and how the development process will take place. This in combination with its open, interactive character instills some "by me, through me, for me" awareness in all participants. Furthermore, taking end-users' perspective as a vantage point has a motivating effect because it provides a clear mission: "why and for whom are we doing this".

Because of the opportunities to realize one's own ideas in a professional setting, *bliep strongly attracted young entrepreneurs. Jesse van Doren, one of them, shares: "At some point we had so many fans who were all talking about *bliep with their friends that we received daily requests from people wanting to work for us. Some were even begging! At that point, we wondered: 'Can't we do something with that?' We divided the large group of fans and interested youth over ten regions, and appointed a community manager for each region. Throughout the country, these communities started working together. Each community had about ten to fifteen youth in it – roughly 150 people in total. They provided us with continuous feedback and a steady stream of new ideas." Wieringa adds: "The structural collaboration with youth made the work so much fun! Had we been 'just another' telecom provider waren geweest, I would have lost interest quickly. What we did at *bliep worked because the youth we attracted were not only talented, but also passionate to give their best contribution."

Efficiency

Because the process does not allow for decisions based on not-validated assumptions, repeating phases or steps is not necessary. That prevents wasting time and money.

In an interview with TheCoCreators co-founder Jochem Wieringa admits that *bliep did not engage in complete co-creation from the start. "In the beginning we just did classic concept testing. We, the grown-ups, had created a few concepts and wanted to check these with our target group youth. Well, they rejected our concepts without mercy. We had to start all over again! That was when we realized that we – even though we weren't that old yet – had grown pretty far apart from our target group. We decided to never ever create things for them, but always work with them from beginning to end. That decision has saved us an incredible amount of time. Working directly with the target group, we would catch mistranslations of their needs at an early stage. Thus, our co-creative development processes were faster than we were used to in our prior work for a large telecom provider."

Result

The co-created solution optimally suits end-users' needs and wishes, which on the longer term leads to results that go beyond just the financial aspects, such as spontaneous word of mouth and end-user loyalty.

*bliep was break-even within three years. That is remarkable in the telecom industry. Jochem Wieringa explains: "We never spent a cent for advertising in traditional media, yet grew with around 8000 clients per month. That was because our clients felt that *bliep was sincere. Thought and run by people like them, with a passion to make their world better."

Organizing large-scale, interactive sessions

It is a functional habit for the Co-creator to regularly unite all directly and indirectly involved internal and external parties in large, interactive sessions. Objectives of such sessions always include 1) providing everyone with an update on the process, 2) motivating people to part-take in the co-creation trajectory, and 3) overcoming potential barriers. These sessions are also good occasions for a joint celebration of success.

The first large-scale, interactive session is the kick-off session. Other logical moments for organizing such events are: the presentation of research outcomes, the presentation of the concept, and the launch of the co-created solution. These sessions should always provide plenty of opportunity for the participants to exchange experiences and knowledge. In general, having end-users fulfill an active role as presenters has a positive effect on support.[8]

Installing a multidisciplinary advisory council

After the co-creation team has been formed, it is a good idea to invite the other stakeholders and key players to take a seat in a multidisciplinary advisory council.[9] By activating them as independent advisors they will feel taken seriously, will stay well informed, and will be more likely to keep supporting the co-creation process. Moreover, given their expertise, they will probably have useful feedback on the process. Through their network they may also be able to connect the right people at the right time.

Facilitating shared research experiences

Immersion in the world of the end-users is an impressive experience. It is so much more powerful to hear someone saying something or see them doing something, than to read a report! That is why active stakeholder and key player participation in research activities has a strong support-generating effect.[10]

8.   Principle 3 (ongoing) lists tips for an effective kick-off session and describes the positive effect of having end-users perform as presenters.

9.   Principle 1 (together) deals with the formation of the co-creation team and other groups, such as the multidisciplinary advisory council.

10. Principle 3 (ongoing) deals with the research phase and the active role of stakeholers, key players, and co-creation team in it.

Street research in a Dutch county shows there is work to do for the CJG"

At the start of 2013 a Dutch county asked agency De JeugdZaak to conduct an evaluation of the Center for Youth and Family (CJG). As a preparation phase for an extensive research, the people working in the CJG and the policy advisors of the county conducted a street research in a local shopping center. Armed with a short, semi-structured survey they approached people with children and asked them about their awareness of the CJG and knowledge of its services, as well as their ideas for the CJG to better serve the needs of parents with children. Afterwards, De JeugdZaak moderated a session during which all street researchers shared their observations, made a collaborative analysis, and formed hypotheses for the next research phase. Not only did this first street research yield a lot more information than expected, but it also made painfully clear for everyone how much work they still needed to do in order to raise the awareness and perceived relevance of the CJG for the target group parents with children. During the fieldwork, confronting remarks were made, such as: "Well, they just call you for vaccinations, and when the kids are older they will see the school doctor a couple of times. I don't think the CJG does more than that." Nothing is more convincing than hearing end-userS say something like that during a genuine conversation!

Active participation in research – benefits

Facilitating stakeholders and key players as co-researchers to engage in direct contact with end-users has several benefits. First-hand end-user understanding, owning the challenge, and involvement with the co-creation trajectory are the most important ones. In addition, it saves time and costs, enhances the acceptance of the research and its outcomes, and increases the motivation to act on results. Although not everyone will be eager to participate, after the fact most participants are usually very positive about their experience.

JIP Noord – the alderman goes on a field trip

As part of the co-creation trajectory leading to the founding of JIP Noord, the Co-creator organized a field trip. She invited the involved policy advisors, employees of partner organizations, the alderman responsible for the local youth policy, and a bunch of local youth for a visit to the successful JIP in The Hague. This eclectic group of people traveled together in a rented bus with driver. The trip offered plenty of opportunities for stakeholders, key players, and local youth to exchange ideas about a youth information point. After arrival at the destination, the questions that the youngsters asked of the manager and employees of the JIP in The Hague were revealing of their perceptions and ideas. Afterwords, the alderman stressed that her direct contact with local youth – not just during this field trip, but also during the various update-meetings – were of huge value to her.

❝ Going on a field trip with all involved policy advisors, the alderman and the target group itself – in this case a bunch of local youth – is not only a lot of fun, but also very revealing!"
Astrid Krikken, former senior policy advisor Amsterdam-Noord

Active participation in research – overcoming barriers

Stimulating people to engage in research is not always easy, especially when they are not used to direct contact with end-users, and when these have a very different lifestyle or age than one's own peers. The following actions[12] can help overcome potential barriers:

- organizing a workshop 'Observing and Interviewing' as a preparation for direct end-user contact;
- facilitating end-user contact, for instance during field trips;
- planning the Key Insight Generator sessions well in advance;[13]
- planning the presentation of research findings well in advance.

When active participation in research is not suitable

Participants in a complete co-creation trajectory can carry out varying research tasks. These include conducting and reporting desk research, participating in an intensive customer-insight-trajectory, and carrying out quick checks by means of an online survey or street research.[14] In those cases there is always a combination of a research objective and an objective with respect to creating or maintaining support.

When the research objective is more important than the support objective, it is a good idea to involve an external specialist for more objectivity, reliability and validity. This may be the case when research results are politically important, or when they are needed to support a decision about a large investment. In that case, participants in the co-creation trajectory will not play an active role as co-researchers. It is, however, still important to involve them, for instance by having them respond to research briefings and proposals, questionnaires and interview checklists, and by inviting them to attend fieldwork whenever possible.

11. Stefanie Jansen, then affiliated with de JeugdZaak, was involved with this case.

12. Principle 3 (ongoing) describes each of these actions.

13. The Key Insight Generator consists of one or more sessions in which participants exchange fieldwork experiences and verbalize the key insight together. Principles 3 (ongoing) and 7 (value-driven) provide more information.

14. Principle 2 (with end-users) describes these research activities.

15. Principle 1 (together) explains the puzzle principle.

Sharing decision-making processes

Support for decisions made over the course of a co-creation trajectory follows from understanding them. That is why transparency about the decision making process is vital. Right from the beginning of the trajectory, the Co-creator needs to manage expectations by 1) clearly indicating the decision making protocol, and 2) how and to what extent participants in the co-creation trajectory can exert influence. This will be different for each trajectory, depending on the extent to which the initiating organization can let go of the need to control the process.

According to the puzzle principle, all participants in a co-creation process are equal, and everyone is responsible for investing their best, unique contribution.[15] Only after all ideas have been gathered and processed, a decision can be made concerning next steps. When the initiating organization is the sole capital investor, it is acceptable that they have the final say. However, when the co-creation trajectory is financed by several partners together, or by an external source (for instance crowdfunding), a dominant stance of the initiating organization in any decision making process will not be acceptable to the other participants. This is also true for decisions that are not traceable as a result of non-transparent communication.[16]

Continuous communication about the process

For creating and maintaining support among stakeholders, key players, and co-creation team it is important for the Co-creator to provide continuous updates on the process. This can happen during large-scale sessions as described above, but also during smaller gatherings, including meetings of the co-creation team, opportunity work groups, and advisory council.

To also keep people in the loop who do not frequently attend live meetings, it is necessary to spread regular updates via other channels. Think social media, email, and mobile. When the initiating organization intends to carry out co-creation trajectories at a regular basis, it may be worthwhile to invest in creating a multi-media platform, enabling the continuous sharing of information and building of ideas by many different parties.[17]

> ❝ It's important to keep senior leadership involved in all stages of the idea creation process. It's best to get them involved right from the start, as they are the ultimate decision makers who have the ability to green light —or kill —a plan. In making these kinds of decisions, there's no substitute for personal consumer experience."
> David Rubin, U.S. Marketing Director for hair care at Unilever[18]

Making and sharing an implementation plan

The implementation plan is a concrete action plan for optimization and implementation of the co-created solution.[19] Linked to it, is the formation of various opportunity work groups that will use the plan as a guide for their parallel activities.[20] Clarity about taks and steps is a prerequisite for a supported process, and a thorough, always up-to-date implementation plan provides this. The Co-creator will make the structure for the plan. Placing people and specific actions in it, is done with the co-creation team and other people participating in the fine-tuning phase. The Co-creator is the one overseeing it all, keeping the plan up-to-date, and celebrating every step that has reached completion. The plan is accessible for everyone, including people who are only passively involved in the optimization and implementation of the solution.

Giving compliments and rewards

It is safe to assume that people who are only passively involved – for instance members of the advisory council – will expect nothing but appreciation for their contribution. Thus, it is important to explicitly honor these people during large-scale sessions, publicly thanking them, possibly with a present of some kind. In addition, it is important to show them appreciation throughout the co-creation trajectory by simply giving them compliments and referring to their valuable contribution in update-emails or newsletters. Finally, a nice gesture is to always take care of excellent catering during their meetings, or perhaps hold some of the meetings in a good restaurant.

On the other hand, members of the co-creation team and opportunity work groups are expected to invest a relatively large portion of their time in co-creation process. Thus, it is imperative for their ongoing support that the Co-creator negotiates time with their managers.[21] In comparison, end-users and independent experts may be rewarded with money, things or services.[22] Naturally, members of the co-creation team and opportunity work groups, too, need to frequently hear compliments and receive other signs of appreciation in order to stay motivated.

Highlighting the puzzle principle

Highlighting the puzzle principle right at the start of a co-creation trajectory and regularly

16. Principle 5 (transparent) deals with the importance of openness in communication.

17. Principle 5 (transparant) describes the various actions to keep everyone in the loop.

18. In an interview with online magazine http://bit.ly/2y3K046

19. Principle 3 (ongoing) deals with the implementation plan.

20. Principles 1 (together) and 3 (ongoing) explain more about the constitution and function of opportunity work groups.

21. Principle 4 (productive) stresses the importance of sufficient time for participants.

22. Principle 1 (together) deals with rewarding external parties. Principle 2 (with end-users) deals with rewarding end-users.

referring back to it during the process helps with creating and maintaining support.[23] When participants of multi-disciplinary teams are convinced that they can add a unique perspective, unique knowledge, and unique skills, they will be motivated to work together towards the best solution. To further stimulate support among involved parties that are not part of a multidisciplinary team, it is a good idea to show how the puzzle principle works in practice. Newsletters and presentations can be used to illustrate how people with very different backgrounds can enrich one another's contributions in a unique way.

When technology expertise is not enough

Over the course of her career, Laura Taylor, Director of Design Exploration at Philips Lighting, has witnessed many innovation processes from within. She was willing to share her key learnings in an interview with TheCoCreators. One of the things she stressed is the importance of 'getting out of your bubble' and establishing close relationships with relevant external parties. "So, you might be a world expert in your technology, but you need to become an expert in the context in which it will be applied. That's why we turn to experts in their particular field who can view a given scenario with different perspectives. It also means involving your customers and end-users because they are the experts on their specific situation! You have to leave your desk and go where your target group is. This is a fundamental element of good design." She adds: "Not only external parties can offer relevant knowledge or a unique perspective. Companies also need to follow a co-creative approach internally. Design, scientific research, marketing, etc., are all specialties in their own right, but they need to work together to create desirable, seamless, and memorable experiences. In order to stay on top of our game, teamwork, collaboration, and knowledge sharing are very important."

Organizing monitoring sessions after launch

After launching the solution, it is important to keep the co-creating partners involved to some extent. That means that in addition to monitoring the performance of the solution with end-users, regular update-sessions with other relevant parties should be conducted in the follow-up phase.[24] During such sessions, results from tracking research and themes from user councils and social media analyses can be presented, as well as new challenges that may give rise to new co-creation trajectories. Ideally, end-users will attend (part of) these sessions, so that they can exchange their views and experiences directly with the other attendees. Always reserving a few chairs for end-users is a healthy habit.

Keeping stakeholders and key players involved after implementation of the solution will increase their goodwill and patience with the solution. Even though positive results tend to show almost instantly for solutions developed in complete co-creation, it is always possible for the target to not be reached right away. IIt would be a pity if that would cause decision makers to prematurely pull the plug, when a clear rise in sales and a positive evaluation by end-users may still be present.

2. How to overcome barriers against supporting complete co-creation?

Organizations that refrain from engaging in complete co-creation or quit during the process, usually give reasons related to lack of money, capacity or time. Another barrier may be the conviction that end-user involvement will disturb the creative process. Some of our clients' quotes:

> *Now we just want to do it ourselves, not with those youth again. That always takes extra time."*
> *Policy advisor during a co-creation trajectory with youth*

> *"Nice proposal, but can't we just do a desk research instead of co-creation? Those things have already been invented; we don't need to do that again...?"*
> *CEO in response to a project proposal*

> *"I don't think it is necessary for me to work with consumers directly; I am a designer, not a market researcher."*
> *Designer at the start of a co-creation trajectory*

> *"I would rather just do an online survey asking the most important questions, so that we can start implementing as soon as possible."*
> *Marketing manager during an orienting meeting*

> *"Why would I give end-users an active role in the organization? They will only be in my way, I have better things to do."*
> *Owner of a software company*

Superficially, a lack of time, capacity, and money can indeed prevent complete co-creation from happening. At a deeper level, other things may play a role. These can ultimately be traced back to a lack of conviction. Any organization can streamline inefficient or

23. Principle 1 (together) explains the puzzle principle.

24. Principle 3 (ongoing) deals with monitoring sessions and tracking research during the follow-up phase.

unnecessary activities to free up time, capacity, and budget for a complete co-creation process. However, they will only do so when the belief that complete co-creation will bring success is stronger than the fear of change.

The cost barrier

It is not uncommon for the Co-creator to first have to overcome a cost barrier before he can start a co-creation process. To accomplish this, he may want to compare the budget of a complete co-creation process with a realistic budget of a standard trajectory. He may also cut the co-creation trajectory into pieces and try to receive a go per piece, or use both of these strategies.

Comparing the budgets of complete co-creation and a standard development trajectory

A standard development trajectory is a process during which end-users and other relevant parties may be consulted, but are not structural partners. Such a trajectory may yield concepts faster than a process of complete co-creation, but these concepts tend to have less end-user relevance. That may only become apparent during the first concept test, or at the market test of a prototype. In that case, the phase of concept development needs to be re-done entirely. Besides extra time, this will take extra resources. When making a realistic budget of a standard development trajectory, these unnecessary loops back into the process need to be included.

VISION

Co-creation as a more efficient and effective alternative to standard innovation processes

Laura Taylor, Director of Design Exploration at Philips Lighting shared her thoughts on complete co-creation as an alternative for standard innovation processes with TheCoCreators: "A frequent and well applied co-creation approach can help steer innovation activities and get to a more relevant product or application, quicker and more efficiently. By working in 'end-to-end co-creation', certain costly and distracting errors are avoided." According to Taylor, the biggest enemies of new product creation are convictions based on wrong assumptions. "It's best to check those very early on, rather than spending a ton of money to build something based on these assumptions (and spend even more to validate them), only then to find out too late that there is something wrong. Often, at that stage it is not even clear anymore as to the 'why'. Talking with customers and experts at every stage of the innovation process avoids having to go back to the drawing board late in the process." As another money and time spender, Taylor points to insights being 'lost in translation'. "While it is convenient to hand over a research activity to someone else it is not very effective for designing the user experience. Anyone who needs to take decisions that affect the proposition and user experience needs to be involved in the research and to hear from customers firsthand."

When compared with a standard development trajectory, the costs of a complete co-creation trajectory can be a relatively high in the early phases. This may be the result of a more thorough customer-insight-trajectory or the development of a dedicated online community. However, in the end, a complete co-creation trajectory is likely to be cheaper, since it needs less, smaller or no formal consumer tests, and inefficient and expensive loops back to prior phases are rare. Moreover, with buzzing by participating end-users already happening during the creative process, costs for communication and promotion can be kept relatively low.

The merits and pitfalls of adopting co-creation as an organizational principle according to Blink

In an interview with TheCoCreators, Jorien Castelein, Director/co-founder of Blink, and Ron Huntley, Team Leader Co-creation, discuss their experiences with being a co-creative organization. As early adopters, they have firsthand experience with its merits, but also thoroughly know its pitfalls. Jorien kicks off: "Embracing co-creation is not a walk in the park. As a new publisher, we had the luxury to do it from scratch, and build our entire organization around students and teachers as our end-users. That does not mean that working end-user-centered is, by now, a piece of cake for us. It will always be difficult to look and listen in a truly open, unbiased way. And it will always take courage to view our own ideas with brutal honesty, and to let go when they don't do what they were supposed to do – even if we already invested a lot of effort and love in them.."

Ron adds: "You have to be willing to keep asking the same questions over and over again: 'What did I see and hear?' 'What did you see and hear?' 'What do our observations mean?' At the same time, you have to suppress the urge to say, and even think things like: 'I know enough now.' Or: 'I have years of experience with this target group; I really know them inside-out.' Or: 'This user is N = 1, not representative of the target group.' "

Ron explains a potential pitfall: "Co-creation means an ongoing search to what you didn't know and its causes. Keeping an open and curious attitude like that takes courage, patience, endurance, and most importantly: a never-ending passion for the target group. If you don't love kids, you won't be able to keep it up, and you may start using the target group to legitimize your own ideas and solutions. When that happens, you need to stop and reconsider what you are spending your money on." Jorien responds to the money-aspect: "A much quoted benefit of co-creation is that it would save money. In a way, this is true, since it will save costs associated with steps back into the development process, or outright flops. When you co-create, you may discover in an early stage – long before market launch – that you are at the wrong track. That will save time. But in the end, I can't say that co-creation will always make your development processes cheaper, at least not for Blink as a content organization." Ron: "Serious co-creation means accepting a relatively large budget for 'unforeseen', and structurally planning extra time for revision. After all, you want to do something with the target group feedback! The reward and added value are in a higher market share, and that is a result of making relevant products." Jorien wraps up: "The smile on the face of your end-user. A solution that really works. If that's what you're after, then co-creation is what you're looking for, and you will find that despite its challenges, it is wonderful and addictive!"

Placing the realistic budget of the standard trajectory (including the loops) next to that of the complete co-creation trajectory will help the Co-creator to explain that complete co-creation is the most cost and time efficient, 'lean' way to the best solution.[25] Moreover, as complete co-creation usually delivers a perfect translation of concept to solution, it will yield maximum relevance for the end-users – in other words it maximizes the chances of success. Finally, the high involvement of all participants during the process means that automatically, learning on the job takes place. This will cause following co-creation trajectories to go smoother.

Trying to get a go bit by bit
Should all of the arguments above suffice to pass the cost barrier, the Co-creator may cut the process into smaller pieces, and negotiate a budget per piece. Thus, he may first obtain a go for a market analysis, then for a customer-insight-trajectory, then for a for a co-creative concept development trajectory, then for the development of a business case, and finally for the optimization and implementation of the co-created solution.

The capacity barrier
To counter the capacity barrier, it helps to make the required capacity in FTE's tangible. A co-creation trajectory tends to activate more employees of an organization than a standard trajectory. And although some may spend (a lot) more time than they would in a standard trajectory, not everybody will participate with the same intensity. Moreover, the frequent loops in a standard trajectory will cost extra time, which means that in reality, such a trajectory will need more capacity than originally budgeted for. Finally, the capacity needed depends on the organization's ambition. Are they aiming to become a co-creative organization, it is a lot higher than when they just want to experiment with one co-creation trajectory first.[26]

Co-creative organizations need an internal Co-creator with a Co-creation Assistant, who should both be able to spend at least 24 hours a week on running the organization's parallel co-creation trajectories. Larger organizations may consider installing a team of internal Co-creators and Co-creation Assistants. Given enough time, an investment like this will pay

---

25.   More information about the concept 'lean' can be found here: http://www.sixsigma.nl/wat-is-lean

itself back by a growing relevance of the organization's offer for end-users, resulting in more and more loyal customers. However, not all organizations have enough reserves to justify such an investment.

Experimenting with a first co-creation trajectory does not need an investment like that. It suffices to temporarily free up someone for two or three days a week to function as the Co-creator on the project, and arrange support for this person with the existing administrative or facilitating department. Alternatively, an external Co-creator can be hired on a project basis. In addition, internal key parties need to be partly freed up for participation. For some, the time investment will only consist of a few meetings, while others will spend at least one day a week for as long as the project runs.

The time barrier

Although a complete co-creation trajectory can roughly be divided into five phases (founding, finding, forming, fine-tuning, and following-up), it is impossible to predict the exact duration of each phase.[27] That is because complete co-creation is not a standard filling in assignment, but a creative process in which the outcome of each phase determines the next. That is an efficient way of working, not allowing for unnecessary steps that are carried out simply because they have been planned. The focus is not on sub-goals and targets, but on the end-goal: the solution that is to be co-created in response to the challenge at hand.

Working with an adaptive planning for development processes is rapidly gaining popularity, and has gotten a big impulse with the trend of agile processes.[28] At the same time, many traditional organizations are still used to a rigid, linear planning, and may feel insecure in its absence. Faith that the unpredictable process of complete co-creation will eventually lead to success is necessary to start and keep going. Thus, it is important to find a sponsor in the top. When the CEO is a believer, anything is possible! The Co-creator can do several things to help overcome the time barrier.

Comparing the duration of complete co-creation with the standard trajectory

Usually, a complete co-creation process will not run longer than a standard development process and in fact may even take shorter. As a result from the extensive market and target group exploration, the early stages of a complete co-creation may take relatively long. Concept development may take quite long as well, since every idea will receive serious attention.

26. Co-creative organizations structurally follow the seven principles of complete co-creation. More information on co-creative organizations can be found in the introduction of this book.

27. Principle 3 (ongoing) deals with the five phases of complete co-creation.

28. Principle 3 (ongoing) mentions agile processen such as Scrum.

Once the concept has been delivered, the fine-tuning phase tends to go much faster than in a standard process. The concept not only has high relevance and appeal to the end-users, but can also count on stakeholder and key player enthusiasm. That will ensure a smooth optimization and implementation process, without large steps back. The Co-creator will make this tangible by placing the Co-creation trajectory and the standard development trajectory above one another on the axis of time.

Complete co-creation (top) versus standard trajectory (bottom) on the horizontal axis of 'time'

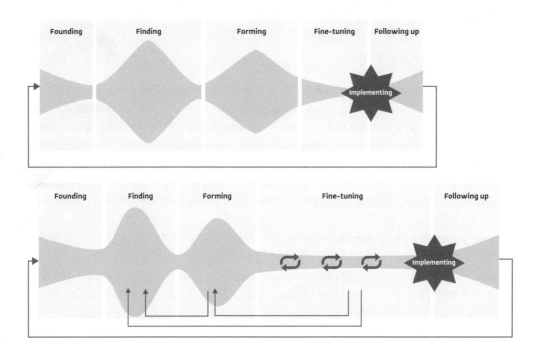

Plan ahead what can be planned

The Co-creator can definitely plan a deadline for completing the research phase. A thorough research, mapping market and target group, can be finished within two weeks if it is only desk research. If the team also wants to talk to end-users as part of a qualitative research, at least four weeks should be planned for preparation, fieldwork, and analysis. This is because recruiting and talking to enough end-users usually takes at least three weeks. Moreover, the Co-creator can pose a deadline for delivering a co-created solution at the end of the fine-tuning phase. Even though such a deadline usually will get changed in the face of reality, the fixation of it on the calendar can prevent stakeholder nervousness and will help motivate the co-creation team to keep going. Where to place this deadline depends on many factors, including the complexity of the solution to be co-created, the amount of time and resources available, and the work culture of the initiating organization (nine-to-five mentality versus working around the clock).

Finally, the Co-creator can plan a few moments for preliminary reports and presentations. Even though it is impossible to specify beforehand what exactly will be reported, planning these update-moments ahead of time may give stakeholders and key players a sense of control.

Positioning the co-creation trajectory as a semi-independent start-up

In trying to realize a loose planning within an organization used to linear projects, the Co-creator may want to position the co-creation trajectory as a semi-independent start-up, operating outside of the established protocols of the organization. This will give it the status of an experiment that does not have to comply with the organization-wide procedures, nor time-consuming political games.

Pitching a phased planning

When a go for a loose planning is out of reach, a phased planning may be a feasible alternative. First, the Co-creator will plan the research needed to answer the question whether the challenge is real and not yet satisfactorily tackled by competitors. If this is so, he can propose a planning for the concept development phase. After the concept has been approved of, he may try to obtain a go for the planning of the optimization and implementation process.

We have witnessed several cases where a similarly phased planning lead to the implementation of a solution. However, the conclusion of every step comes with the risk of a no-go. Thus, it is always best to shoot for approval of the loose planning for the entire co-creation trajectory.

The creativity barrier

A frequently used argument against a co-creative approach is the conviction that end-users are not able to think in an innovative way, are not creative, or may disrupt the creative process. Yet time after time we meet end-users that are perfectly capable of thinking out-of-the-box! This is particularly true for children and adolescents, but also for other target groups. Often, the ultimate solution for the challenge at hand is literally conjured up by an end-user.

Even if the assumption that end-users are not creative were true, this would not be a reason to keep them outside of a development process. After all, the main reason to co-create with end-users is to guarantee the relevance of solutions for them. An organization that starts involving representative members of the intended target group as co-developers will find that their input fundamentally differs from the input of other parties, including target group experts. This is because end-users themselves are the only experts with respect to their experience of the organization and its offer. They can provide unique insight about this experience, which – especially in combination with the other parties' expertise – will inspire the group to deliver out-of-the-box ideas with ultimate end-user relevance.[29]

The best way to tackle the creativity barrier is to have stakeholders and key players work directly with end-users. It is best to start with a brainstorm session in which end-users participate in addition to the usual participants. Make sure the moderator is experienced and comfortable leading an eclectic group of people. Then, sit back and have reality convince the skeptics. They will learn first-hand that truly opening up for end-user input, means receiving essential inspiration!

> " Projects in which I share the table with consumers and make sketches of their reactions and ideas on the spot give me a lot of energy and inspiration. These processes can seem chaotic, but it is exactly that uncontained energy that leads to wonderful and out-of-the-box ideas. Often better and more inspiring than the rigid briefings and processes I get from large corporations."
> Art-director at a design agency

Fear of the unknown

An overwhelming amount of research literature shows that humans are creatures of habit, afraid of breaking with existing patterns and habits.[30] The deeply ingrained needs for predictability and control cause us to hold on to that which is known, even when it no longer serves us. Committing to complete co-creation may involve letting go of traditions that have led to satisfactory results for decades. That may evoke fear, which can be intensified by a lack of experience with complete co-creation and not knowing any success stories.

> " When I applied for the function of marketing manager with an educational publisher, I asked them whether they had ever discussed with children how they learn best. The interview committee looked at me as if I had just insulted their mother. 'No, we aren't used to working that way,' they said. I was not surprised I didn't get the job."
> Marketing manager at a business-to-business publisher

The best remedy against fear of the unknown is sharing best practices and organizing co-creation experiments, allowing people to get used to it in a safe setting.

Fear of losing control

The initiating organization will only be able to allow complete co-creation to unfold when it can let go of control over the process. After all, equal collaboration as an important characteristic of complete co-creation can only unfold when there is no dominant party. Letting go of control can be a no-go, especially for traditional organizations. They may experience this as the exchange of overview and (supposed) insight for a blind trust in an unpredictable process with an uncertain outcome.

As a remedy against this fear, the Co-creator can try to position the co-creation trajectory as a semi-independent start-up, a strategy that has been described before. It may be easier for stakeholder to lean back and witness an experiment taking place outside of the organization and its rules and habits. If this is not an option, the Co-creator may choose to settle with the 'voice-of-customer model' as a semi-co-creative approach, whilst trying to prepare the organization for complete co-creation.[31]

The voice-of-customer-model

Organizations battling the fear to lose control may opt for the 'voice-of-customer model', sometimes labeling it co-creation. They do involve end-users and other relevant parties in the development process, but keep full control over the process and its outcome. Thus, end-users and other parties are not equal co-developers, but function as inspirers and evaluators. Organizations regularly use a similar approach as a marketing tool, since brands 'for and by people' tend to get positive free publicity. However, despite a potential positive marketing effect on the short term, this approach seldom leads to the long-term, sustainable success that tends to follow from a process of complete co-creation.

When the Co-creator recognizes that stakeholders do not fully embrace co-creation, but are leaning towards the voice-of-customer-model, he can either try pitching complete co-creation as the way to go, or settle with their preference. If he chooses the latter approach, it is important for him to make explicit that this is not complete co-creation. That prevents drawing conclusions about the efficiency and effectiveness of co-creation when in reality, only the voice-of-customer-model has been used. Moreover, the clarity about the process will generate support among the involved parties. If they expected to be part of a complete co-creation process, the voice-of-customer-model may have a negative effect on their motivation. After all, they have only been brain picked. When they know this beforehand, they can make an informed decision whether or not to participate.

29. Principle 2 (with end-users) deals with the topic of end-users in creative settings.

30. More information about human beings as creatures of habit can be found here: Earls, M. (2007). *Herd - How to change Mass Behaviour by harnessing our true Nature*. Hoboken: John Wiley & Sons.

31. Principle 1 (together) discusses getting an organization ready for complete co-creation.

Opposing stakes

The challenge should have direct relevance for the co-creating parties. That means they are sharing a motivation to conquer it, even if they are very different in terms of backgrounds, experience, and views. By keeping the common mission top-of-mind, a shared sense of working together on an important challenge will emerge, coupled with a strong driver to work together in realizing the best possible solution.

Should the various participants in a co-creation trajectory aim to realize opposing objectives, support for the trajectory will disappear like snow under the sun. More or less secretly, they will each do 'their own thing'. Implicit or explicit sabotage of the co-creation endeavor will be the result of such hidden agendas.[32]

CASE 59

Working on the CJG (Center for Youth and Family)

Between 2007 and 2010, The Netherlands were actively building the CJG's (Centers for Youth and Family). These were meant to be low-threshold physical locations where parents and children could ask all of their questions about raising healthy, happy children. Annemiek van Woudenberg, author of the book 'Werken aan het CJG' (Working on the CJG), spent those years helping various Dutch counties with the realization of a CJG. She always aimed to not only involve all parties that would have to collaborate within the CJG – such as organizations for youth public health and parent support – but to also give voice to parents and children as end-users of the CJG. In an interview with TheCoCreators she says: "What I noticed was that the CJG would only be successful when we got all chain partners to replace their organizational stakes with the joint responsibility for the wellbeing of local children, youth, and their parents. That is not easy to accomplish, and we didn't always succeed. Yet when we did, we would get into a flow and would have a working CJG in no time, because everyone would share the same driver: the passion for healthy and happy local children and youth." Van Woudenberg still believes in something like a CJG. "Such as shame that the political agendas have been changed in the meantime and that the CJG does not get the attention it deserves.."

A co-creation process can clearly show that one of more of the collaborating organizations is no longer relevant for the solution, or needs to structurally change in order to play a for end-users relevant role in it. In such cases, an urge may surface to place continuity of the organization above the importance of real value-creation. To overcome this barrier, the Co-creator needs to create a safe atmosphere and start a dialogue between all parties. It is essential for all of them to first be entirely open about their stakes and then commit to a shared goal.

> " In my work I see many different parents every day. They always complain about how they can't find their way in the local arena of services with respect to raising children and youth public health. I viewed the CJG as a great solution for this problem: one recognizable point where all needed expertise in this field is bundled. On paper, the GGD (public health service) was a key partner in the CJG. As a youth health care physician working for the GGD I wanted to help build it. However, my manager did not allow me to spend any time co-developing the CJG. She was afraid that the CJG would replace the GGD, and that youth public health would suffer degradation. An irrational fear if you ask me, but that attitude of the GGD did cause our local CJG to never really take off... And everything is still confusing for the parents. It was a very disappointing experience for me."
>
> *Youth health care physician in a small Dutch county*

Given the destructive effect of multiple (hidden) agendas, it is recommended to start a co-creation trajectory with a signed manifesto, stating the shared objectives. When several organizations take part in the process, it is best to make this official, at least as a covenant, but better yet as a mandatory contract signed by all parties.

3. Questions to our readers

1. If there is currently a challenge within your organization that is suitable for a complete co-creation trajectory, how would you describe it (within two minutes) to a lay person?

2. Imagine you want to pitch this challenge with stakeholders.
a. Which internal and external stakeholders can you think of?
b. What do you view as the most important reasons each of these stakeholders would have to reject complete co-creation, and how could you help them overcome their resistance?

3. Imagine you would have to form a co-creation team to tackle this challenge with.
a. Which parties would you want to add to make sure that all relevant points of view are represented?
b. How would you establish support in the co-creation team for both the challenge and the process of complete co-creation?

32. Principle 5, (transparent) discusses the importance of open communication during complete co-creation.
33. More information about this book can be found here: http://bit.ly/2x7zSv7

Principle 6: Supported.
Complete co-creation is supported
by all involved parties.

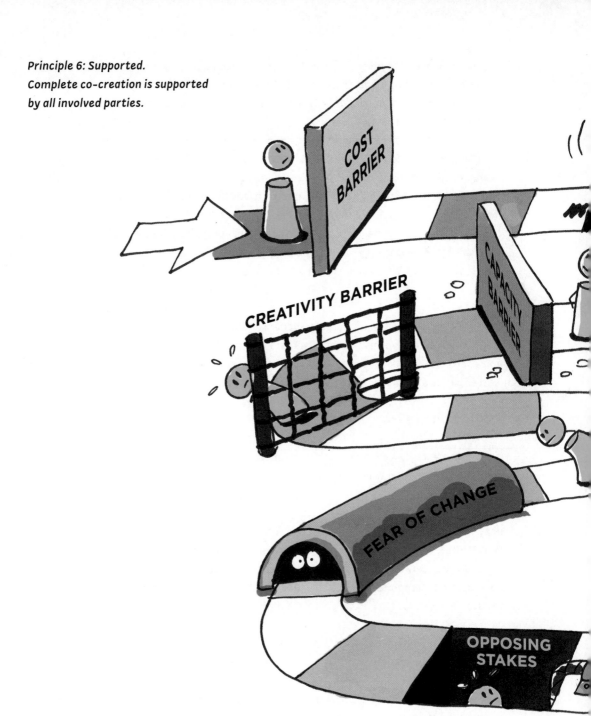

TIME BARRIER

SUPPORT FOR:
COMPLETE CO-CREATION
THE CHALLENGE
THE SOLUTION

Complete co-creation results
in value creation for end-users,
the involved organizations,
and the planet.

PRINCIPLE 7
VALUE-DRIVEN

Today's organizations are under pressure. Establishing and maintaining end-user loyalty is getting more and more difficult, finding and keeping good personnel is getting tougher, and the call for accountability is rapidly getting more urgent.[1] In this light, it is not surprising that a growing number of organizations embrace co-creation as an organizational principle. These co-creative organizations take transparent, productive collaboration with end-users, employees, and other relevant parties as their starting point for decision making.[2] Inspired by the wish to add to a sustainable society on this planet we share, they always aim to realize value at the end-user level, the organizational level, and the global level.

In every step of their development processes, co-creative organizations keep track of the involved parties, the ways and extent to which each one of them played their part, how value was created, what decisions were made by whom and why. Thus, it is easy for the higher management to give *vertical* account to the other employees, and it is equally easy for these organizations to give *horizontal* account to external parties and end-users.[3]

> ❝ *In most innovation processes, teams are fixated on building 'something', like a product or an app, because that is where they feel comfortable, whereas they should be focused on understanding the drivers and barriers of their target group in context. Only they can they create a meaningful solution for a real challenge – one that truly brings people further. This may encompass developing a total experience, including less tangible elements like customer engagement. Whether people are ready to work this way is as much a question of mindset as competence."*
> *Laura Taylor, Director of Design Exploration at Philips Lighting*

> ❝ *Clean air, water, and a livable climate are inalienable human rights. And solving this crisis is not a question of politics, it is a question of our own survival."*
> *Leonardo DiCaprio, Actor and producer[4]*

Reading guide principle 7 – value-driven

This chapter discusses the three levels of value creation according to the following questions:

1. How do co-creative organizations create value on the level of end-users?
2. How do co-creative organizations create value on an organizational level?
3. How do co-creative organizations create value on a global level?

Again, we will start with the case JIP Noord and end with three questions to our readers.

1. In this chapter, we only briefly discuss the trends and shifts that are causing pressure on organizations.
    The introduction to this book deals with them in more detail.
2. The concept of 'co-creative organizations' has been introduced in the introduction to this book.
3. More information about taking horizontal and vertical account can be found here: http://bit.ly/2f0nd3e
4. Quote from: https://www.leonardodicaprio.org/

JIP Noord, value-creation at three levels[5]

End-user level: By taking the needs of local youth as a starting point for the development of JIP Noord, an appealing service was created for this target group. The key insight was that youth feel they do not have any problems, just questions, mostly about practical stuff. By focusing JIP North on answering questions and offering practical advice and guidance for low-threshold topics such as work and internships, it has established itself as a safe and useful place for youth to swing by. Once inside, they may feel comfortable enough to ask other types of questions as well. For those who are too shy to step by, reach JIP Noord can help anonymously by WhatsApp, a very popular service that is relatively often used for questions about heavier subjects like violence, sexuality, and drugs.

Organizational level: Aside from taking youth as end-users seriously, from the very beginning, people from various organizations that were to carry out JIP's services, were highly involved in the development process. This instilled a sense of ownership of JIP Noord among these parties. Having seen youth's response to the center and its services as it evolved, they are convinced of its value for the local youth and acknowledge its preventive power. Thus, they feel that they are part of something good and important, and are intrinsically driven to contribute.

Planetary level: For politicians, prevention of more serious problems is a popular topic for conversation and agenda-setting, but in the end they tend to spend most of their attention (and budget) on reaction, rather than prevention. This is because their popularity is directly related to their ability to solve acute problems. That is concrete, measurable, visible, and easy to communicate about.

In contrast, preventing problems that have not yet occurred is abstract, invisible, hard to measure, and difficult to convey. What did JIP Noord save society in terms of money and problems? How many youth have – in part because of their contact with JIP Noord – *not* become victims of violence, how many have *not* been raped, stolen from, or faced debts? How many youth did *not* catch an STD, did *not* get hooked to addictive drugs, did *not* radicalize and did *not* drop out of school? And how many of them did *not* become homeless, criminal or unemployed? These things are impossible to grasp in hard numbers.

Yet it is clear that JIP Noord has a preventive effect. The affiliated organizations indicate that since the opening, they have seen and spoken with a lot more youth from all walks of life about topics like the ones listed above than ever before. Moreover, a large number of youth received information and advice about such topics through WhatsApp, something that was not possible before. Concluding, we can say that JIP Noord definitely has a positive effect on a piece of our beloved planet.

---

5.   More information about this case can be found in the introduction of this book.

6.   Principle 2 (with end-users) discusses the concept of 'key insight'. Principles 2 and 3 discuss how to get to deep customer understanding and key insight.

1. How do co-creative organizations create value on the level of end-users?

End-users are increasingly critical and only stay loyal to products, services, experiences, and brands that hold real value for them. Thus, in the co-creation paradigm, value-creation at the level of the end-users equals to the right to exist. This boils down to filling in a real need for a specific target group. Working from key insight is a prerequisite for doing this.

Developing a powerful key insight

A key insight follows from a deep understanding of the drivers and barriers of a specific group of people to show certain behavior. Deep target group understanding can't be found in the office, unless the target group consists of office employees. The only way is going out there and immersing in their world.[6]

> " *At Unilever, we go straight to the consumer to gather insights that will lead to breakthrough ideas and communication. We believe in immersing ourselves in their culture to better understand them in ways that will allow us to not just market to them but to add value to their lives, creating products they need and want. It's critical to get personally down-and-dirty in this process; focus groups and quantitative research have their place, but are in no way replacements for first-hand, direct, consumer contact. Sometimes you may have to travel to find an insight and sometimes the insight or idea may be right next to you."*
> *David Rubin, U.S. Marketing Director for hair care at Unilever[7]*

We use the following definition for the concept of key insight:[8]

▸ **A key insight is a deep driver for a target group, powerful enough to inspire new behavior.**

In this definition, 'new behavior' refers to behavior that is desirable in light of the challenge at hand. As an example, consider the challenge "finding new trainees for our trainee-program". In this case, the desirable behavior of the target group 'potential candidates for our trainee-program' might be 'visiting a recruitment event'. The key insight should be a deep driver that – when activated in relation communication about this event – will give a candidate just that little push he or she needs to sign up.

---

7.   In an interview with online magazine Forbes: http://bit.ly/2y3lFwH

A strong key insight reflects the target group's perspective, is positive, universal, and possible to own, and passes the 4R-test.

Reflecting the target group's perspective

Should the target group be confronted with the key insight, they would say: "Yes, that is totally me!" That is why it is a good habit to write a key insight in the target group's language, in a sentence starting with 'I'. Furthermore, using motivational language helps to express a target group's deepest drivers. Verbs like 'to aim', 'to strive', 'to need', 'to wish', 'to seek', 'to want', 'to enjoy', 'to love', etc. work well in a key insight. "Knowing that I am taking good care of my family makes me feel powerful," is a strong key insight. "The need for affirmation that they are taking good care of their family is a strong driving force for many men," is the target group understanding underlying this insight.

Positive

"Parents don't give their children enough boundaries," is an example of behavior that is labeled as problematic and needs to be changed. Problematic behavior can be a good vantage point for developing a valuable brand, product, service, experience or communication. However, directly translating the problematic behavior into a key insight is usually a bad idea. That is because problematic behavior is linked to a negative self-image. People identify with positive self-images rather than negative ones, and are prone to ignore messages linked to their negative selves. Thus, any product, brand, or communication based a 'problem insight' runs the risk of getting ignored.

Thus, it is best to phrase a key insight in positive terms: "I want to raise my children in harmony." Or: "Sometimes I just need peace." Instead of: "I have a hard time saying no to my kids." Only in specific instances do key insights phrased around negative scenarios work well. This is true, for example, for themes where one's own erratic behavior may negatively impact the wellbeing of another person. "I don't want to be the cause of somebody else's death," is a strong insight that could inspire a successful campaign promoting safe behavior in traffic.

Universal

A key insight is a universal driver for a target group. That means it seldom refers to a product, service, or brand. After all, propositions about products, services, or brands hardly ever represent a deep, universal truth for a substantial group of people. "I love coffee," is, for example, a less universal driver than: "Sometimes I really need a clear mind." Or: "I immensely enjoy a moment just for me."

8.   This definition, including the other information in the paragraph on key insights, is loosely based on a presentation by Oxford Strategic Marketing from 2006, combined with practical experience of the authors of this book.

Possible to own
Although a key insight does not have to refer directly to a product, service, or brand to be relevant for it, it does need to be possible to own. The two insights above with respect to a clear mind and a moment 'just for me' can both be owned by the product coffee. It is up to the brand to choose one as the base of the brand personality.

Finding a key insight that can be owned in a unique way by a product, service or brand does not necessarily mean searching for a unique insight that has never been used before. The general kids insight "I love building new things," has been successfully claimed in unique ways by various brands in the history of construction toys, and is there to use for any future brand of construction toys. Similarly, many brands of personal care products for babies and young children have found their own, unique way to claim the universal parent insight "I want to take care of my child in the best possible way," and there may be many more to come. After all, 'the best possible way' to care for a child can take an endless amount of forms, depending on the target group.

The 4R-test
The 4R-test helps to establish the power of a key insight and consists of the following four questions:

· Is the insight a reality for the end-users?
· Is the insight relevant for the end-users?
· Does the insight resonate with the end-users?
· Does the insight evoke a reaction with the end-users?

The R of reality
A powerful key insight is a deep truth for the target group. That means it can only follow from deep target group understanding.

> 66 *When seeking direct contact with end-users it is important to 'shut down' one's own ideas and experiences, and be open like a child. Just experience all that can be seen, heard, smelled, tasted, and felt in the end-users' world, without interpreting or judging it."*
> Dieneke Kuijpers, Managing Director WPG Kindermedia

The R of relevant

Realistic insights can be more or less relevant for a target group. For instance, the key insight "I want to feel healthy," is realistic and relevant for most seniors, while their adolescent grandchildren are probably not really driven by it. Most adolescents do like to feel healthy, so the insight does fit their reality. However, the insight will lack relevance for most of them, because humans at that age usually do not have any chronic health issues. Thus, a campaign highlighting the short-term effects of working out – such as losing weight, gaining muscle, getting a better condition and feeling energized – will have more impact among adolescents than a campaign focused on intangible longer-term health effects, like diminished risk of heart disease.

The R of resonating

Resonance means that when a string is touched, it will keep vibrating. In other words: a good insight does not only give rise to the intended behavior on the short term, but also on the longer term. For the target group 'active seniors', the insight "I want to feel healthy," is likely to inspire lasting changes in behavior. Motivated to keep up their active lifestyle, but confronted with the effects of aging, they may develop a new yoga or power training habit, may start taking daily supplements, or try anti-aging personal care products. Resonance thus refers to both initial and lasting behavior change.

The R of reaction

Activating a powerful key insight will evoke the intended behavior: entering that store, becoming a member of that club, wearing that seat belt, studying at that school etc. Should a realistic, relevant insight be triggered without linking it to a specific product, service or brand, end-users may display varying behaviors. Activating the insight "I need a clear mind" without relating it to (a certain brand) of coffee may inspire someone to go for a walk in the park or take a smart drug. Thus, it is important to activate the key insight whilst linking to the target behavior.

From key insight to relevant solution

When the co-creation team has phrased a powerful key insight that passed the 4R-test, it is time for the development of concept starters. The key insight is leading in this process. The decision which of the concept starters will be developed into a full-on conceptual solution is partly based on the extent to which the concept starters fit the key insight. Once the solution has been delivered, various opportunity work groups will prepare it for launch. The key insight guides this phase as well, so that the solution and potential introduction campaign will be perfect translations of target group needs.[9]

9. At this point we will just give a summary of the development process; principle 3 (ongoing) describes it in more detail.

"I Kandoo it" – example of a development process inspired by a powerful insight[10]

For parents it can be pretty stressful to teach a young child how to wash their hands, wipe their butt, wash their hair etc. Somewhere around 2004, Procter & Gamble must have defined this stress as a business opportunity, and probably went searching for a solution. This is more than likely how Kandoo came to be – a product line for the personal hygiene of young children. Kandoo products include foamy soap and wet toilet paper.

In no way have we been involved in the development of Kandoo. Therefore, we don't know if this is really how it started. However, based on our private and work-related knowledge and experience with the target group young children in relation to Kandoo, we can make a tentative analysis. We enjoy doing that, since Kandoo is a beautiful example of how a powerful key insight can lead to a product line that actually improves the end-user's life – in this case making it easier and more fun. We believe that Kandoo has been developed from the positive self-image of young children that they are already 'big kids' that can do things on their own. In addition, we think that the team developing Kandoo, was taking into account the understanding that parents' positive self-image includes raising their children in harmony (as opposed to: with temper tantrums, which can be intense with a toddler).

We infer that the kids-insight and slogan "I Kandoo it" was the starting point for the development of the entire Kandoo product line. Kandoo products and packaging always stimulate young children to do it 'by my own self'. For instance, the Kandoo soap pump is not only particularly easy to use for small hands, but is also a bright green and purple funny looking frog, that spits out extremely foamy soap with a strong, fruity odor.

Furthermore, we believe that the parent-insight "I want to stimulate my child's independence in a fun way" (or something similar) gave rise to the marketing platform. TV-commercials show cute toddlers proudly performing personal hygiene tasks, such as washing hands. Mailings contain handy, funny looking sticker systems to help parents with the potty training. On the website www.kandookids.com, parents can download positive child-rearing tools, such as a potty training chart, and they can find tips and information about the personal hygiene development of children.

As a brand, Kandoo offers clear guidance for the development of all kinds of products that would stimulate young children's independence with respect to personal hygiene by adding fun value. We would say that products that don't do this – for instance something which calls for full control by a parent or expert, like a hair dressing set – do not fit. The same is true for a product with a packaging that kids find unattractive, since this will fail to inspire them to doing it independently. In other words: such a product would fail the "I Kandoo it" test.

10. The analysis of Kandoo in this chapter is based on desk research combined with our personal understanding. As we were not able to get a hold of the person within Procter & Gamble responsible for Kandoo, this analysis has not been verified with Procter & Gamble. Thus, it serves a purely illustrative purpose.

"Say 'no' more often" – example of a development process following a flimsy insight

'Say 'no' to children who are eating too much and moving too little, otherwise twenty percent of our children will be too fat in five years.' This was the motto that SIRE[11] took as a starting point for developing a communication campaign targeted at parents (December 2004). The campaign included a movie with gloomy music, picturing a sad looking child's head placed on various obese, adult bodies. A child's voice-over told parents that they should not think too lightly of obesity, and should say 'no' more often.[12]

The campaign was conceived of in a brainstorm session consisting of various experts, including target group experts, communication experts, nutritional experts, and market researchers. Although some of these experts were also parents, among the brainstorm participants were no typical members of the intended target group, parents with children at risk of becoming obese.[13] The target group understanding of the participating experts must have been something like: 'These parents have a hard time setting boundaries for their children with respect to developing healthy behaviors.' It seems that they took this understanding as the inspiration for the campaign and refrained from phrasing a strong key insight appealing to the self-image of the target group in a positive way.

The 'say no more often' campaign did not have any diminishing effects on the incidence of childhood obesity in The Netherlands: in fact, since 2005 it only increased.[14] Yet, the campaign probably did sort some effects. At a subconscious level, the music and images may have evoked feelings of depression among viewers. They may have formed a subconscious link between this negative feeling and SIRE, a so-called 'unintended communication effect'. At a conscious level, the communication may have struck a chord with people agreeing with its message – for instance childless people who feel parents should be more firm with their kids and parents who are already saying 'no' often to their offspring. However, the intended target group is likely to have kept the communication from affecting their consciousness. After all, this is how people operate: needing to feel good about ourselves, we are attracted to communication that confirms a positive self-image, while blocking communication undermining it.

SIRE might have reached a different outcome had they translated their target group understanding into a positive key insight as their starting point. For instance: "I want my children to grow up in a healthy, yet fun way." This may have led to the development of a platform for and by parents – possibly endorsed by professionals – filled with practical tips for stimulating health-promoting habits among children in a positive way. Think practical tools to playfully teach children about healthy habits, techniques to distract their attention from unhealthy options, tips and tricks to make healthy options more appealing, health challenges for families and friend groups, etc.

11. The abbreviation SIRE stands for: Stichting Ideële Reclame, the Dutch Foundation of Idealistic Advertising.

12. Watch the movie here: https://www.youtube.com/watch?v=HYquE_e-e0Y .

Left: Kandoo's original frog packaging, and right: SIRE's child with obese adult body

 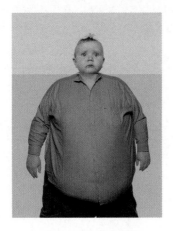

2. How do co-creative organizations create value on an organizational level?

Organizations are dealing with an intensifying battle for good personnel, as well as with fierce competition, coming from unexpected places. In order to survive, they need to become sources of inspiration for employees and relevant external parties. In other words: they need to engage in value-creation at an organizational level.

The flourishing organization

In the co-creation paradigm, a flourishing organization offers end-users exactly that which serves their needs, and they are doing this in a way that not only feels good for the employees and business partners, but also comes across as likeable for outsiders. An organization will flourish when it structurally invests resources and positive energy in itself, its employees, its business partners, and the end-users.

We choose the term 'flourishing', rather than 'growing', because in the co-creation paradigm, the aim for growth is not the same as the creation of value. In this paradigm, it is possible for a stable, not growing organization to hold a lot of value for its employees (or co-owners), the end-users, and the planet. In contrast, the sole focus on growth of the past decades has not led to the creation of sustainable value, but instead to a lot of unnecessary products, trash, pollution, and stress. In the end, our planet and its inhabitants are served best by the development of products and services that are focused on creating a sustainable society on planet Earth. This may coincide with growth, but it does not have to.

Co-createIKEA: co-creation on a global scale

IKEA believes in co-creation and understands that the journey ahead is an inclusive one. Thus, the organization has sent out an open invitation to the world to co-create a 'better everyday life'. The aim is to solve challenges for people as well as our planet, together with customers, co-workers, suppliers, designers, students, researchers, and many more. "We think it is crucial that innovation happens in collaboration with the market, as well as everywhere in IKEA. With co-createIKEA we want to open up our product development, collaborate and activate the collective mind," says Mikael Ydholm, Communication and Innovation Strategist at Inter IKEA in an interview with TheCoCreators. "From the beginning of 2018 IKEA will launch an online co-creation platform open to all IKEA FAMILY members and roll it out country by country during the coming years. We will also work with start-ups and some universities in order to find untapped potentials to explore innovative ideas, and we will co-create with existing communities and labs around the world to exchange new ideas and learnings." In addition, IKEA will set up a maker space: "This will be a creative area in the prototype shop at IKEA, where all different parties can meet and work on future products and innovations together." Ydholm is not afraid of sounding overly ambitious. With enthusiasm, he concludes: "It's a worldwide program, but we will launch it step by step. With millions of loyal IKEA customers, it is going to be big!"

So, if – in the co-creation paradigm – growth is not the primary predictor of success, then what is? We would phrase the answer to this question as: the capability to adapt. Rigid organizational structures and business models no longer work in the co-creation paradigm. Instead, flourishing organizations are adaptive organizations.

The investment of resources

The primary goal of a flourishing organization is value creation, not profit maximization. However, for flourishing to occur, sufficient resources need to be available to invest in the organization, the employees and business relations, the development of expertise, new products or services, and the marketing of these. These resources can be realized by making a profit or attracting funds, for instance by applying for subsidies, accepting gifts or engaging in crowdfunding. Since working according to the seven principles of complete co-creation maximizes the chances of loyal end-users, doing so may help evoke trust among fund keepers.

13.   We know this because at the time, Stefanie Jansen was working at kids market research agency KidWise, and heard about this brainstorm session from a colleague, who participated as a target group expert. However, since we did not take part in the brainstorm and have only heard about its outcome indirectly, we have written about it in a hypothetical form.

14.   See for instance: http://bit.ly/2fav7L6

Investing in synergy

The positive relationship of an organization with the end-users, business partners, and other external parties, expresses itself in goodwill. End-user goodwill does not only pertain to the intention to stay a loyal client, but also to the willingness to help the organization become even more valuable. Similarly, business partner goodwill pertains to the willingness to add a useful contribution, not in order to get the very best deal today, but rather to add to the organization's sustainable value so as to still be able to make mutually enhancing deals tomorrow.

Within the co-creation paradigm, money is no longer the most important factor to take or keep a job or to secure a certain deal or not. The central driver is the 'higher' experience of overlapping ethical principles and synergy within parties that complement each other, resulting in sustainable value-creation at the levels of organization, end-users, and planet.

3. How do co-creative organizations create value on a global level?

The ego-centered orientation of the prior decades is steadily making place for a 'we-orientation'. While shareholders are increasingly asking organizations to take account for their actions, citizens are organizing themselves to stand up against socio-economical inequality. The pressure on politicians and organizations to change their ways in order to preserve our planet is quickly intensifying.

CASE 64

Avaaz, a world-wide movement for societal co-creation[15]

Avaaz was founded in 2007 and wants to unite citizens from all countries to narrow the gap between the current and the ideal world. Primary active on social networks, Avaaz enables millions of people to take low-threshold action on pressing themes such as climate change, human rights, animal rights, corruption, poverty, and conflict. As opposed to good causes such as Green Peace, Avaaz does not have a top-down approach with a pre-fixed agenda. Rather, the organization works bottom-up by offering members a platform where they can indicate the themes they find important. On the one hand, Avaaz bases its actions on input from the members, while at the other hand it is facilitating members to start their own actions. By September 2017, Avaaz counted more than 45 million members. The organization has booked countless successes, such as convincing Pakistan's government to install a scholarship program that allows three million children growing up in poverty to go to school.

In the power paradigm, organization-driven management is linked to success, while in the co-creation paradigm this is true for value-driven management.[16] The ongoing shift from the power paradigm to the co-creation paradigm comes with a progressive broadening of the organizational scope from short-term profits to a longer-term perspective, inspired by the realization that we all share responsibility for our planet and its future inhabitants.

Organization-driven management

The central driver behind organization-driven management is claiming a right of existence based on market dominance. This comes with a hierarchical organizational structure and a reward system stimulating a short-term profit orientation. Accountability flows 'bottom-up' from the work floor to the higher management and shareholders. Employees are not encouraged to express their views on the organization, but are managed to accomplish assignments that follow from a fixed task description. The organization may seek contact with end-users as respondents in traditional market research, but does not take them seriously as co-creators. Furthermore, the premise that external parties are not to be trusted makes it difficult to engage in flexible partnership. Organization-driven management is more concerned with the continuity of the organization than with the creation of sustainable value.

Value-driven management

The central premise for value-driven management is that organizations only have a right to exist when they are relevant to their end-users and the world at large. In their ongoing mission to create short-term and long-term relevance, these organizations take their employees, end-users, business partners, and other relevant parties seriously as sources of insight and ideas. These synergistic relationships are characterized by continuous vertical and horizontal accountability. Value-driven organizations are more concerned with creating sustainable value than with securing their own continuity. Thus, they are flowing with the market in an open, fluid way, continuously transforming and always seeking new connections and partnerships in order to optimally serve the end-users.

15. More information about Avaaz can be found here: www.avaaz.org.

16. The introduction to this book explains the CoCreationTransitionModel, which shows the current shift from the power paradigm to the co-creation paradigm.

17. More information about Natura can be found here: www.natura.net and here: http://bit.ly/2fnL5yb and here: http://bit.ly/2juAhmh and here: http://www.relatoweb.com.br/natura/13/.

Natura Cosméticos as an example of a value-driven organization[17]

Natura Cosméticos, founded in 1969, is the second-largest cosmetics brand in Brazil. In 2011 Forbes ranked it as the number eight most innovative organization world-wide, right after Apple (5th) and Google (7th). Alessandro Carlucci, the executive president of Natura Cosméticos, views the contribution to a better society as his organization's right to exist. Wellbeing, environmental consciousness, sustainability, and transparency are Natura's central values. The yearly report always offers a long list of social and ecological goals and an evaluation of the extent to which these have been fulfilled.

From organization-driven to value-driven

The organization-driven orientation fits our timeframe less and less well. The traditional hierarchical structure and focus on organizational continuity make it difficult (if not impossible) to respond fast, yet effectively to challenges in the market. More and more this truth presents itself: change is a necessity for survival!" => "... yet effectively to challenges in the market. Organizations realizing this can opt for a sudden, radical transition to a value-driven orientation. More often, though, they make a passive choice for a long and unplanned process of change. This process can be divided into seven phases: 1) success, 2) the tearing of success, 3) fixing or pretending, 4) attacking, dodging, or distracting, 5) reputation damage, 6) financial damage, and 7) transformation (or bankruptcy).

The seven phases of organizational transformation

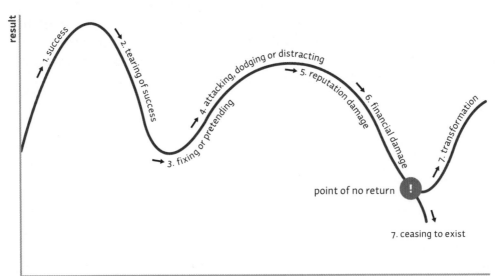

From success to the tearing of success

Many large corporations are still reaping the fruits of their market dominance. Like large oil tankers, they are pushing forward on the momentum of a course they set long ago. However, their success is showing tears: knowledge is leaking away, and their leading position is under constant attack. Ever more frequently, these tankers are meeting unpredictable storms on a sea that used to be free of ripples. Large as they are, they cannot respond in a swift and adequate way. As opposed to the smaller ships sailing 'their' sea in increasing numbers, they suffer from damage or may even capsize. Although it would be smart for these tankers to transform, preferably into a fleet of agile ships, many will first focus on damage control.

> ❝ *Anyone at Tesla can and should email/talk to anyone else according to what they think is the fastest way to solve a problem for the benefit of the whole company. You can talk to your manager's manager without his permission, you can talk directly to a VP in another dept., you can talk to me, you can talk to anyone without anyone else's permission. Moreover, you should consider yourself obligated to do so until the right thing happens. The point here is not random chitchat, but rather ensuring that we execute ultra-fast and well. We obviously cannot compete with the big car companies in size, so we must do so with intelligence and agility."*
> *Elon Musk, CEO of Tesla[18]*

Fixing or pretending

Organization-driven management tends to respond with quick fixes to challenges in the market. Examples are: placing more responsible products next to the existing assortment, developing new varieties of the classic best seller, and playing with the P's of price, place and promotion. In addition, these organizations may pretend they are adopting a value-driven orientation, for instance by installing a client council or broadcasting a story with respect to corporate social responsibility.[19] A popular form of pretending is 'greenwashing': communicating the positive effect of certain environmentally friendly activities, while staying silent about other activities' adverse effects on the environment.[20]

Quick fixes tend to work for only a short time. Critical consumers will see through them, and soon enough the organization may meet the same problems they were trying to fix. At that point, they can try fixing it again, or they may resort to attacking, dodging, distracting or transforming.

18. To read more about what Elon Musk said: http://bit.ly/2x6UlzU

19. CSR includes environmentally friendly organizational processes and humanitarian activities.

20. On www.greenwashingindex.com campaigns are ranked on the extent to which they engage in 'greenwashing'.

McDonald's applied some quick fixes[21]

In 2004, the American film-maker Morgan Spurlock did an experiment on his own body, documenting it in the movie "Supersize me". On a mission to show how detrimental the SAD (standard American diet) is, Spurlock decided to live on McDonald's food for thirty days straight, and to always say 'yes' in response to the question whether he wanted a larger portion (the so-called 'supersizing'). Moreover, he limited his daily exercise the level of the average American. As a result, Spurlock gained more than eleven kilograms and developed all kinds of side-effects, including a high cholesterol level, mood swings, sexual dysfunction, and a fatty liver. It took him fourteen months on a strictly vegan diet to lose the extra weight.

Six weeks after the release of this movie, McDonald's canceled the super size option, developed communication of healthier options, and made the Happy Meal healthier. Whether these changes are direct reactions to the movie or not, McDonald's actions appear to have been quick fixes, trying to change an increasingly negative image.

Attacking, dodging, and distracting

Organizations may attack by means of law suits or price wars. They may dodge by finding new markets with less critical consumers to buy their existing products, for instance the Second and Third World. Distracting happens when an organization acquires new branches – preferably organizations that are embraced by critical end-users – partly to generate income that way, but mostly to distract attention from the problematic core business.

The music industry attacks... and reinvents itself[22]

In the music and entertainment industry a worldwide battle has been going on for years. While producers are trying to protect their rights on content, music lovers keep finding new platforms for the free downloading and sharing of that content. Stichting Brein (the Brain Foundation) focuses on protecting the rights of the Dutch entertainment industry. This has lead to various legal disputes and lawsuits against (online) suppliers of free content. After facing steadily diminishing revenues since 1999, in 2012 this negative tendency in the music industry turned around.

This can't be attributed to the industry's warfare, but to the successful exploitation of the markets for online streaming, paid music services, and download stores. In other words, the music industry has reinvented itself and this generates new income.

Nestlé is dodging (on a boat in the Amazon)[23]

With stagnating markets in Western societies, multinationals in the food industry are focusing on developing so-called emerging markets. The Swiss corporation Nestlé has been increasing its activities in the Brazilian Amazon area. Here the company's floating supermarket is reaching new consumers, who are mainly buying processed foods like snacks, candy, and infant formula. As a result, local inhabitants are starting to replace their traditional foods like rice, beans, free-range meat, and home-grown vegetables with ready-to-eat options, and are increasingly opting out of breastfeeding their babies. At the same time, these areas have witnessed a huge increase in obesity and diabetes.[24]

With the acquisition of companies such as Innocent Drinks, Coca Cola is engaging in distraction[25]

In 2013, Coca-Cola raised its stake to over 90% of the shares of the British company Innocent Drinks. The Innocent juices and smoothies based on pure fruit had been a big hit in Europe for years. Since the take-over, Innocent has introduced a range of new products with varying rates of success. These include bars, ready-to-eat meals, and fruit drinks mixed with mineral water.

For Coca-Cola, this has not only been a profitable acquisition in terms of money. The concern has also used its new branch to create a more positive image by stressing the investment in healthier options. However, the soft drink Coca-Cola is not getting any healthier, and the concern keeps pushing this product, as well as its other soft drinks, mainly in the Second and Third world.[26]

By agreeing with the take-over, Innocent Drinks is part of a growing list of companies that used to start out small and independent, passionate to offer a better alternative for the products produced by multinationals, only to finally become part of these same large corporations.[27]

21.   More information on this McDonald's case can be found here: http://cbsn.ws/2ycVVyS

22.   More information about developments in the music industry can be found here: http://econ.st/2y3xSS0

23.   More information about Nestlé's boat in the Amazon can be found here: https://bloom.bg/2x7EgtN

24.   See also the 2012 documentary "Way Beyond Weight" about overweight Brazilian children.

25.   More information on Innocent can be found here: Wall Street Journal Blog, 22 Feb 2013 and here: http://on.wsj.com/2x7nLy3

26.   More information about Coca-Cola can be found here: http://bit.ly/2fp4Y0L

27.   See for instance the black list of Real Food For Life: http://bit.ly/2fb49Ts

Reputation damage and financial damage

We expect that on the longer term, strategies such as attacking, dodging, and distracting will lead to a more rapid loss of end-user loyalty. On the short-term, organizations may succeed in finding large groups of less critical consumers, potentially realizing large profits that way. Ultimately, though, the critical mass will increase social pressure, for instance by placing the organization on a black list. This will make the organization increasingly unattractive as an employer and as a business partner. It may also result in a decrease of the organization's credibility as a conversation partner for governments. Finally, the organization's value will diminish, forcing it to reinvent itself (or go bankrupt).

CASE 70

Beef Products Inc. will have to reinvent itself[28]

In 2011, the popular British cook Jamie Oliver exposed McDonald's for using a pink substance in its meat products. This with ammonium hydroxide treated paste of meat particles is also referred to as 'pink slime'. Not long thereafter, McDonald's announced that it had ceased using this substance. In addition, Burger King, Taco Bell, Wal-Mart, the American supermarket concern Safeway, and several other American supermarket chains quit selling meat products made with this ingredient as well. In response, Beef Products Inc., an American company producing the infamous paste of meat particles, closed three of its four factories, and fired hundreds of employees.

Transformation

From the adage "If you can't beat them, join them!" an increasing number of organizations are adopting a value-driven orientation. It is never too late to take this step. Transformations that take place after a long, dark period of organization-driven management are particularly inspiring to end-users and other relevant parties!

True transformation is only possible by going back to the core question: "Why are we here?" and coming up with a meaningful answer that carries the three levels of value-creation that carries the three levels of value-creation: end-users, organizations, and planet. From an organization-driven orientation, it may be easy to answer the question who or what an organization is, but not why that is valuable for whom. The key to relevance, credibility, and sustainable success is in the answer to the why-question.[29]

---

28. More information on pink slime can be found here: http://nydn.us/2xEzvJV and here: https://usat.ly/2jxtyIy

29. Watch Sinek's popular TED-presentation about the 'why' here: http://bit.ly/2vYKER1 More information on his book *Start with Why* can be found here: www.startwithwhy.com.

30. More information about Dave's Killer Bread can be found here: www.daveskillerbread.com, here: http://bit.ly/2jxNQ4H, and here: http://bit.ly/2y3xmTV

From a drug using criminal to Dave's Killer Bread[30]

In the markets for personal development, health, and spirituality, it is a rule that the most successful gurus must have overcome addictions, criminality or near-death experiences in order to convincingly sell their products and services. A parallel is visible in other markets. The story of transformation sells! Take for instance Dave's Killer Bread, a product line of super healthy breads that has been taking the American supermarkets by storm since 2005. On his website, Dave shares in detail how, from a depressed adolescent, he became a drug using criminal and ended up in jail time after time, until he got locked up for a longer duration in 1997. During that period, he was able to transform himself by making music, art, and taking antidepressants. When he left jail in 2004 he stayed away from the drugs, and started working in the family bakery in Oregon. There, he developed the product line Dave's Killer Bread, organic breads that are produced by ex-inmates, filled with healthy seeds, and free of trans fats and genetically manipulated ingredients.

Replacing an organization-driven orientation with a value-driven one requires depth, self-insight, power, and courage. That is because an organization, in its quest for a meaningful answer to the why-question, needs to expose itself. The organization needs to show unhappiness with the current orientation, express the wish to change, and ask end-users, employees, and potential other relevant parties to help create sustainable value. TTo then structurally realize transformation of the management style requires entering a process of continuous shifting; getting stuck in self-research is not an option. The five phases of complete co-creation can act as a guide to this path of change.[31]

4. Questions to our readers

1. How would you describe the 'why' of your organization?
a. To what extent do you think your answer matches the vision of the higher management?
b. Which aspects might be different?

2. Describe a specific target group relevant to your organization. This can be an internal target group, such as a department, or an external one, like a certain type of end-users. What might be a key insight for this group?

3. Describe the value that your organization is currently creating on the levels of 1) end-users, 2) organizations, and 3) the planet.

31.   Principle 3 (ongoing) introduces the five phases of complete co-creation.

Principle 7: Value-driven.
Complete co-creation results in value creation
for end-users, the involved organizations,
and the planet.

VALUE CREATION AT AN ORGANIZATIONAL LEVEL

VALUE CREATION AT THE LEVEL OF THE END-USERS

VALUE CREATION AT A PLANETARY LEVEL

WIN MORE DEALS

POWERFUL INSIGHT

SUSTAINABILITY

WIN MORE WAY

EPILOGUE

by Olaf Hermans & David Pinder (*)

Thank you, Maarten and Stefanie, for a clear and relevant exploration of why and how complete co-creation is a strategic and actionable imperative for each customer-centric organization.

You draw a legitimate fault line between co-creation and other useful forms of customer or user focused action like service design, focus groups or voice-of-customer programs. The value outcomes of these initiatives are indeed different, both for the customer and for the organization. The key reason behind that difference is that customer co-creation is built on relational premises ("providing value in relation with the customer"), whereas most other forms of customer interaction resort under the exchange or delivery paradigm ("providing value for the entitled customer"). The value that customers derive from being heard and understood, is totally different compared to the value that customers derive from being in a relationship and having contributed. Increasing customer value does not always mean that organizations need to work harder and customers want to pay less. Involved customers, often those in an ongoing relationship, see value in having the best of an organization or even in working with the organization to create the best. Customer centricity is nothing more than continuously dialoguing with customers and organizing together for their preferred type of value.

As customer co-creation research started around 2005, customer co-creation experts already explore its future. Next generation co-creation strategies, methods and technologies will move co-creation beyond being the form of crowdsourcing that allows the co-development of solutions, products or services for groups and the individuals in those groups. We would like to point to three key (r)evolutions we see emerging in the co-creation domain.

First, the object of co-creation will not be limited to products, services or solutions. Its object will become single processes, including single interactions and encounters. Co-creation will become an integrated process with any other "host-process" that need some form of co-creation: collaborative design, co-enactment, customization, or transformation.

Each business process will dispose of a proprietary co-creation engine that enables co-creation. This implies that in the business and IT architecture of a firm co-creation will move from being a distinct business function to being a platform service which is provided to applications and processes. Co-creation as a Service (CaaS) will be rendered in real-time before, during or after a host-process has started. As most processes in ongoing and customer-centric relationships require co-creation, often with a single participant, there is no limit to the future relevance and scope of co-creation with the customer, and no reason for customers not to participate.

Second, customer co-creation will not be limited to the development function. Rather it will manage all forms of customer role enhancement in an organizational process or business function. Besides being a co-developer, customers or users can co-create in roles as co-producer, quality controller (compliance), participant, engager, citizen, or ambassador. Various levels of engagement and contribution will be distinguished depending on the chronic (attitudinal) or acute (situational) levels of customer interest, expertise and energy. Moreover, various customers will be used for various types of co-creation that require different cognitive skills: e.g. conceptual versus practical behavior; long-term focus versus short-term focus behavior; observation versus sense making/giving; backward evaluation versus forward planning.

Third, as co-creation is a service by the customer and by the organization, both to themselves and to each other, both with extrinsic and intrinsic motivations, there are relational conditions between both that need to be met and maintained before actual co-creation can be effective, efficient and durable. Examples of such conditions are mutually experienced trust, involvement, identification, closeness, and reciprocity. These dynamically evolving relationship states have a direct impact on the way co-creation processes and outcomes will need to be shaped. Today, co-creation platforms too often make simple yet false assumptions about the (high) quality of relationships and (high) level of goodwill between participants.

A lack of information about the state of relationship between co-creators makes it impossible to reliably predict changes in levels of engagement of a participant, loyalty to the outcomes of co-creation, and about participants' drop-out from the co-creation process. Co-creation thus needs its own "loyalty program": ongoing conversation about satisfaction with and value from the relationship. The strategic ongoing relationship conversation ("where do we go from here with process X") includes the voice-of-customer program ("what can we do better for you in process X"), and explicitly includes the discussion about ownership and the co-creative role of the customer in amending a process.

The following table briefly summarizes the current and new focus of co-creation research and development, both in terms of concept, value, methods and supporting technologies.

Current and future focus of co-creation research and development

Co-creation concept

Current focus
The development of solutions, products and services based on an open dialogue between a firm and its volunteering users and stakeholders.

Co-creation warrants the value and competitiveness of an organization's solutions, products and services.

Future focus
The integration of the resources of a firm and the resources of each user and stakeholder in every process and function of the organization.

Co-creation warrants each user and stakeholder to be an endogenous resource of an organization in every touchpoint.

Co-creation value

Current focus
Value is created by the involvement of volunteering users and stakeholders in all steps of the solution, product, or service development and production process.

Value is primarily situated in:
· better and individualized solutions, products and services
· participation in and co-ownership of the development and adoption process
· the enhanced loyalty as a result of such value

Future focus
Value is created by the facilitation of each user and stakeholder in bringing any resource needed to design, co-enact, customize, or transform any process, and such before, during or after the execution of the process.

Value is situated in:

- the optimization of every process of the organization with every customer/user and stakeholder
- the continuity and accuracy in merging organizational and customer resources across all shared service and experience processes
- the enhanced loyalty as a result of such value and of the ongoing strategic conversation in which the actual co-creation process is embedded

Co-creation implementation and work methods

Current focus

In accordance with the 3C model, three functional domains of co-creation were identified:

- customer insight, or the collection, filtering and preparation of relevant data for decision making
- customer connection, or the relationship with and involvement of all relevant parties in various organizational processes
- customer co-creation.

Future focus

Co-creation no longer is a stand-alone process but one that is planted on any host service or experience process. As a result new co-creation methods are:

- **Co-creation differentiated experiences:** Beyond their traditional segmentation based on needs, service and experiences processes now are differentiated based on varying levels of customers' ability and desire to co-create the service or experience process

- **Design for Co-creation:** As co-creation itself is a CX layer ("CX+") that mutually informs the base CX delivery process, a key unit of optimization is the "encounter". A priori set CX deliverables and touch-points will be complemented with open relational and co-creational experiences. Relational experiences drive goodwill, co-creational experiences capitalize on goodwill

- **The meta-experience of co-creation:** ongoing dialogue needs to be shaped that explores the relationship pre-condition for co-creation. Prior to being executed, the assumed next best relational or co-creational actions and questions in the relationship are also subject of this dialogical conversation. Big data analytics needs such conversation before its suggestions and conclusions can be converted into action

Co-creation technologies

Current co-creation technologies
adjust to the current implementation domains, and thus consist of:
- data technologies (collection, analysis and reporting)
- collaboration technologies
- individualized production technologies

Future co-creation technologies
adjust to the new implementation domains, and thus consist of:

- co-creational content management platforms that match co-creational tasks and information to customers' varying levels of goodwill to co-create
- encounter management technologies that warrant the inclusion of relational and co-creational moments in customer journeys
- voice-of-Relationship technologies that generate data on customers' state of relationship with the organization (enabling service systems to contextualize the customer), and that issue orders/tickets for relationship maintenance and co-creation facilitation to the organization whenever customers are ready

(*)
Olaf Hermans (USA) is a cognitive scientist specialized in the mental processes of customers who relate and co-create with service providers. His research team develops interactional intelligence to stimulate customer goodwill, customer role enhancement and customer ownership in service processes and service encounters.

David Pinder (UK) is an international thought leader, consultant and author in the domain of value creation. As a former Accenture consultant he has helped many firms in remodeling their business, their value proposals, and in working their way back to the customer as the pounding heart of value creation and reception.

ACKNOWLEDGEMENTS

We, Stefanie Jansen and Maarten Pieters, founders of TheCoCreators, wrote this book based on five years of intensive desk research, expert interviews, and our own decade-long experience in the fields of market research, concept development, and co-creation. We could not have completed this book without the help of the following academics and professionals:

Alain Raap, André van Dijk, Anne Brevoord, Annemiek van Woudenberg, Arjan Polhuijs, Ashley Culvin, Astrid Krikken, Benjamin Brinckerhoff, Bert van Hoof, Bridget Waters, Brigitte van Teeffelen, Chad Reynolds, Christian Ruane, Cora Kleinhout, Danja Lekkerkerk, David Pinder, Dieneke Kuijpers, Edward Verity, Erik Roscam Abbing, Fatima Fattouchi, Fennemiek Gommer, Frank Janssen, Helene Hartlief, Henrik Stamm Kristensen, Hetty Hurkmans, Jan Willem Roseboom, Jesse van Doren, Jochem Wieringa, Jonathan Turner, Joost van der Plas, Jorien Castelijn, José Manuel Dos Santos, Laura Kamphaus, Laura Taylor, Maria Letizia Mariani, Martine Jansen, Maroof Daud, Menno Tabbernal, Miel Wellens, Mikael Ydholm, Niek Janssen, Olaf Hermans, Partizia Bertini, Paul Thursfield, Peter Guldemond, Peter Polhuijs, Pierre-Yves Panis, Pieter Waller, Puck Jonkers, Rhiannon Beggs, Róbert Bjarnason, Ron Huntley, Rutger Peters, Simon Rycroft, Stephen Ratcliffe, Steve Blank, Sylwia Kleynen, Thomas Troch, and Yvonne Gerridzen.

THANK YOU!

In addition, we would like to express our gratitude to our family and friends, who supported us throughout the process, with a special loving thanks to Kees Jansen and Panghea J. Weinberger. Without the two of you we would still be working on it!